KU-470-490

DELHI AGRA & RAJASTHAN

BY
MELISSA SHALES

Produced by AA Publishing

Written by Melissa Shales

Original photography by Douglas Corrance

Edited, designed and produced by AA Publishing.
© The Automobile Association 1995.
Reprinted February 1998.
Maps © The Automobile Association 1995.

Distributed in the United Kingdom by AA Publishing, Norfolk
House, Priestley Road, Basingstoke, Hampshire RG24 9NY.

A CIP catalogue record for this book is available from the
British Library.

ISBN 0 7495 1016 1

The contents of this publication are believed correct at the time of
printing. Nevertheless, the publishers cannot accept responsibility for
any errors or omissions, or for changes in the details given in this guide
or for the consequences of any reliance on the information provided by
the same. Assessments of attractions, hotels, restaurants and so forth are
based upon the author's own experience and therefore descriptions given
in this guide necessarily contain an element of subjective opinion which
may not reflect the publisher's opinion or dictate a reader's own
experiences on another occasion.
**We have tried to ensure accuracy in this guide, but things do
change and we would be grateful if readers would advise us of any
inaccuracies they may encounter.**

Published by AA Publishing (a trading name of Automobile Association
Developments Limited, whose registered office is Norfolk House,
Priestley Road, Basingstoke, Hampshire RG24 9NY. Registered number
1878835) and the Thomas Cook Group Ltd.

Colour separation: BTB Colour Reproduction, Whitchurch, Hampshire.

Printed by: Edicoes ASA, Oporto, Portugal.

Cover picture: *Taj Mahal*
Title page: *Rajasthani craftsmen waiting for tourists*
Above: *statue of dancer, Menal Shiva temple*

Contents

BACKGROUND ———————— 5
  Introduction   6
  Geography   10
  History   12
  Culture   16
  Hinduism   18
  Islam   20
  Jainism   21
  Politics   22

FIRST STEPS ————————— 25
  Getting Around   26
  Indian Railways   28
  Living with India   30
  Photography   32

WHAT TO SEE ———————— 33
  Delhi   34
  Agra and environs   56
  Ajmer and environs   65
  Alwar and environs   68
  Bharatpur and environs   70
  Bikaner and environs   74
  Chittorgarh   78
  Hadoti region   80
    Bundi   80
    Kota   84
  Jaipur and environs   88
  Jaisalmer and environs   100
  Jodhpur and environs   108
  Mount Abu and environs   116
  Ranthambore   120
  Udaipur and Environs   124

GETTING AWAY FROM IT ALL 139

DIRECTORY ——————————— 147
  Shopping   148
  Entertainment   156
  Festivals   158
  Children   160
  Sport   162
  Food and Drink   164
  Hotels and
    Accommodation   172
  On Business   176
  Practical Guide   178

INDEX AND
ACKNOWLEDGEMENTS —————— 190

Features
Gandhi   24
City Streets   40
The Great Moghuls   54
Peacocks and Parakeets   72
The Rajputs   92
Mud Huts and Millet   114
Project Tiger   122
Perfection in Miniature   130
Each in his Rightful Place   138
Flora and Fauna   142
A Symphony of Colour   154
Chilli and Spice   170

Maps
India in Asia   6
Delhi, Agra and Rajasthan   8–9
Delhi City   35
Delhi – Red Fort   38
New Delhi Tour   46
Old Delhi Walk   48
Many Ages of Delhi Tour   50
Agra   57
Agra – Red Fort   58
Fatehpur Sikri   62
Chittorgarh   79
Bundi and Jait Sagar Cycle Tour 82
Jaipur City   90–1
Jaipur to Amber Tour   98
Jaisalmer   101
Jodhpur   109
Mount Abu   117
Udaipur   124
North from Udaipur Tour   136

Walks and Tours
New Delhi Tour   46
Old Delhi Walk   48
The Many Ages of Delhi Tour   50
Bundi Cycle Tour   82
Pink City Walk   96
Jaipur to Amber Tour   98
Jaisalmer Town Walk   106
The Upper Lakes Tour   134
North from Udaipur Tour   136

About this Book

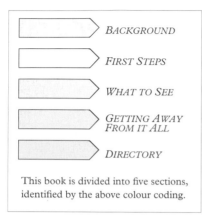

BACKGROUND

FIRST STEPS

WHAT TO SEE

GETTING AWAY
FROM IT ALL

DIRECTORY

This book is divided into five sections,
identified by the above colour coding.

Background gives an introduction to
the region – its history, geography,
politics and culture.

First Steps offers practical advice on
arriving and getting around.
What to See is an alphabetical listing of
places to visit, interspersed with walks
and drives.
Getting Away From it All highlights
places off the beaten track where it is
possible to relax and enjoy peace and
quiet.
Finally, the **Directory** provides practical
information – from shopping and
entertainment to children and sport,
including a section on business matters.
Special highly illustrated features on
specific aspects of the region appear
throughout the book.

A well-earned midday break from working
in the fields

BACKGROUND

'At the dawn of history
India started on her
unending quest and the
trackless centuries are
filled with her striving,
and the grandeur of her
successes and failures.'

JAWAHARLAL NEHRU
First speech as Prime Minister
of Independent India.
Midnight, 14 August, 1947

Introduction

*I*ndia is mellow with the ageing elegance of ancient civilisations; she is raw with the abrasiveness of newly independent power. Heart-stopping beauty and spiritual purity cloak heart-rending poverty and cruelty; physical squalor can hide the souls of saints. She will inflame and overpower the senses, bombarding them with sights and sounds and smells to feast and sicken. She is confusing and frustrating, inspiring and uplifting. You will return home bemused, and whether you loved or loathed the country, you will never be quite the same again.

Nothing here is ever what it seems. The tattiest building can hide inner walls inlaid with precious stones. The man in the cotton pyjama suit may be a clerk or a milkman or a cabinet minister. People weave silk, but prefer nylon; Hinduism counts making money (the right way) as a sacred duty, but successful men freely give up all worldly goods and become wandering *sadhus*.

Delhi, Agra (home of the Taj Mahal) and Jaipur together make up the 'Golden Triangle' as three of India's most visited and fascinating cities. This book also includes the rest of Rajasthan, a tiny corner of India, but as big as many European countries. Until 50 years ago, there were 23 independent kingdoms,

INDIA IN ASIA

THOMAS COOK'S
Delhi, Agra and Rajasthan

By 1870, Thomas Cook was selling steamer tickets to India (£50 First Class; journey time – 30 days). In 1873, teetotal Thomas Cook himself visited India during a world tour, spent an evening with the Temperance Society of the Agra garrison, and promised to send them a library of books to help with the boredom (lest they should succumb to drink). By 1880, the company was setting up a series of guided tours across India – and tours for Indian residents to other areas of the world. The first ran over Easter, 1881. By 1887, they were advertising a wide range of itineraries including stops in Delhi, Agra, Jaipur, and Ajmer. By 1891 the company had set up its first banking services in India, and by 1892 was publishing pamphlets with practical information and details of the major sights for the use of its customers. Nothing much has changed!

Spectacular camel parade during the Jaisalmer Desert Festival

each with a rich tradition of history, art and architecture in great palace cities such as Udaipur, Jodhpur and Jaisalmer. It is also an area of great beauty, from the jungle-clad hills and lakes of the south, home to a wealth of animals, to the deserts of the northwest, where camels are as precious as life. Above all, the people, with their vibrant saris and turbans, heavy silver and twirling moustaches make the area unforgettable. A holiday here will never be totally comfortable, but it will be one of the greatest experiences of your life.

'This is indeed India! The land of dreams and romance, of fabulous wealth and fabulous poverty, of splendour and rags, of palaces and hovels, of famine and pestilence, of genii and giants and Aladdin lamps, of tigers and elephants, the cobra and the jungle, the country of a hundred nations and a hundred tongues, of a thousand religions and two million gods, cradle of the human race, birthplace of human speech, mother of history, grandmother of legend, great-grandmother of Tradition ... the one land that all men desire to see, and having once seen, by even a glimpse, would not give that glimpse for the shows of all the rest of the globe combined.'

MARK TWAIN
More Tramps Abroad (1897)

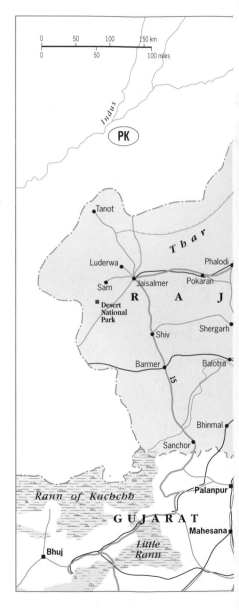

DELHI, AGRA AND RAJASTHAN

Geography

*T*he area covered by this book falls mainly within the vast undulating plains of North India, at 200 to 400m above sea level. Delhi, a Union Territory standing on its own, covering 1,485sq km, and Agra, largest city in the massive state of Uttar Pradesh, both come within the outer limits of the Ganges basin. Rajasthan covers 342,274sq km and divides into two very different landscapes. The southeastern hills are lush, green, well-watered and fertile, with heavy monsoons from July to September. The central Aravalli Hills (maximum height 670m) mark the edge of the Ganges watershed. Beyond them, the land is increasingly flat and arid, eventually melting into the burning sands of the Great Thar Desert, with temperatures reaching a summer maximum of 50°C and virtually no rain.

Population

India has the second largest population in the world, currently estimated at 950 million, of whom 70 per cent still live in rural areas. About 80 per cent are Hindu and 13 per cent Muslim. There are also around 23 million Christians, 19 million Sikhs, 7 million Buddhists, 4 million Jains, and a very few Parsees and animist/pagan tribal groups. Delhi, with a population of about 9 million, is India's third largest city. Around 1.5 million people live in Agra.

Rajasthan, with about 52 million people, is one of the poorest and most backward states in India, with 17 per cent of the population belonging to Scheduled Castes (untouchables), and 12 per cent classified as tribal people (ethnic minorities). Of these, most belong to the Meenas and Bheels;

Yoked oxen draw water from deep wells for village irrigation

The lush, green patchwork of the Aravalli Hills offers a stark contrast to the Thar Desert

smaller groups include nomads. The state still has one of the world's highest birth rates. The average annual income is two-thirds that of India as a whole, as is the literacy rate at 24 per cent.

Economy

Delhi is a world class capital, with all that that entails financially. Agra is a centre for heavy industry, but Rajasthan still has relatively little manufacturing industry. Most workers still huddle in tiny craft workshops, producing fine carpets, jewellery and fabrics. Mining for marble, quartz and silver (as well as semi-precious stones such as jasper and cornelian) has long been a prime source of income. Village subsistence agriculture is being joined by an expansion of cash crops such as pulses, sugar-cane, cotton and millet, thanks to irrigation schemes like the Indira Gandhi Canal. One of the biggest industries of all is tourism.

GREENING THE DESERT

The Indira Gandhi Nahar begins in the Punjab, at the Harrika Barrage on the confluence of the Sutlej and Vyas rivers. It is made up of a main 649km-long canal and nearly 9,000km of branches and minor tributaries. Plans are afoot to extend the main canal a further 135km. Once complete, it will supply Himalayan water for drinking, industry and to irrigate an area of over 1.5 million hectares. It has already halted the relentless expansion of the desert, droughts and floods are being brought under control and with the planting of new crops, Rajasthan's scrubby sands are slowly being transformed into a lush, green paradise. The authorities have even designated an area as a Desert National Park, to preserve a slice of desert ecology for the future (see page 140).

History

2500–1500BC
The Harappa culture – city dwellers, traders and builders – grows out of the earlier Indus valley cultures in north India to become the first significant civilisation on the subcontinent.

1500–1000BC
The first Aryans arrive from the Middle East, bringing with them the chariot, the Vedic religion (the precursor of Hinduism) and the caste system.

6th–5th century BC
Buddhism is founded by Prince Sidhartha Gautam (The Buddha, c 563–483BC) and Jainism by Vardhamana Jnatputra (Mahavira, c 540–468BC), both in north India.

321–185BC
The Maurya Dynasty is founded by Chandragupta. His grandson, Ashoka (c 268–231), conquers almost the entire subcontinent to become India's first emperor. Embracing Buddhism, he then becomes a benign dictator, still revered as a national hero today. His empire fragments on his death.

AD320–535
Chandragupta II (no relation to Chandragupta I) is the next to conquer significant portions of north India, founding the Gupta Empire. It is a golden age of both arts and sciences, brought to an end by invading Huns. The area again dissolves into tiny kingdoms.

8th–11th centuries
In 711 the first Arab invasions bring Islam to north India. From about 750 onwards the Rajputs appear from the west and begin to build up real power across northwest India, although they remain fragmented into numerous small kingdoms who spend much of their time fighting each other (see pages 92–3.)

11th–12th centuries
Increasingly frequent Islamic incursions culminate in a fierce campaign by the Turkish Sultan, Mohammed Ghori. In 1192 he defeats a group of Rajputs led by Prithviraj Chauhan and claims their territory, leaving a trusted slave, now ranked as a general, in Delhi as his governor.

1206–1526
In 1206 Ghori dies and the governor, Qutb-ud-Din-Aibak, breaks away and sets himself up as Sultan of Delhi, founding the Delhi Sultanate or 'Slave Dynasty'. For the first 150 years, Delhi is a centre of prosperity and power. The Islamic Sultanate and the Hindu Rajputs battle it out for the next 320 years.

1398–9
The first Mongol invasion, led by Timur (Timberlane), heir of Genghis Khan, leaves the Delhi Sultans in control of only a tiny area around the city.

1498
Vasco da Gama discovers the sea route to the East and Europe begins to take an interest in India.

1526
Second Mongol invasion. The Sultan of

Delhi, Ibrahim Lodi, is defeated at the Battle of Panipat, and Babur (ruler of a small kingdom in central Asia and a descendant of the great Mongol Khans) defeats the Rajputs at Khanua, and Sultan Ibrahim Lodi at Panipat, creating the Moghul Dynasty (see pages 54–5). In all, there were 17 Moghul emperors, of whom the first six were the greatest. Warriors, builders, garden lovers and patrons of the arts, they created a golden age of Indian culture, leaving north India its most enduring legacies – the great forts of Delhi, Agra and Rajasthan, and that most beautiful of buildings, the Taj Mahal (see page 60). The dynasty survived until 1857 when the last Moghul emperor, Bahadur Shah II, was overthrown by the British for his part in the Mutiny (see page 14).

Late 16th century
Emperor Akbar forms marriage alliances with some Rajput princes, subjects others to ferocious and prolonged warfare, and brings Rajputana into the Moghul Empire as a series of subject states. Only Rana Pratap Singh holds out, in spite of the loss of his great fort of Chittorgarh, fleeing to the mountains to organise a resistance (see page 78).

1618
The British East India Company receives trading privileges from the Moghuls in exchange for protecting their trade routes from the Portuguese. Over the next 50 years British influence gradually fans out across India.

18th century
The Moghul Empire begins to crumble following the death of Bahadur Shah in

1712. The Maratha Empire stretches north and east from the Deccan, reaching the gates of Delhi in 1750 before being defeated by Afghan invaders. By the end of the century, the subject Rajputs turn to Britain for help in getting rid of the Marathas. The ensuing treaties theoretically restore their independence, but in practice the principalities become British protectorates.

The Moghuls were great warriors and patrons of the arts

1773–4
The Regulating Act turns the East India Company into a British administrative agency. Warren Hastings is appointed the first Governor-General of British India. He offers several Indian princes military assistance in exchange for various concessions – effectively setting up puppet states.

1799
Lord Wellesley (later to become the Duke of Wellington) leads a huge military campaign, conquering a great deal more of southern India.

1815–18
The final British conquest of the Marathas. Almost the entire subcontinent is now under the direct rule or 'influence' of the British Raj.

1857–58
The Indian Mutiny is sparked by a false rumour that bullets are stored in cow and pig fat, offending both Hindu and Muslim soldiers. The Rajputs ally themselves with the British. Intense fighting, atrocities and sieges occur on both sides before the British finally gain control.

The last Moghul, Bahadur Shah II, sides with the Mutineers. He is captured in the grounds of Humayun's tomb, tried for treason in the Red Fort, Delhi, officially ousted from power and exiled to Burma. The British Government buys out the East India Company, declaring India to be part of the British Empire, governed by a viceroy and an Indian Council.

1877
Queen Victoria is proclaimed Empress of India.

1885
The first nationalist stirrings. The Indian National Congress holds its first meeting in December.

1906
Foundation of the All-India Muslim League.

1911
Capital of British India transferred from Calcutta to Delhi.

1914–18
Indian troops play an important role in World War I. All political disagreements are put on hold for the duration. In 1915 the political activist, Mohandas Karamchand Gandhi, returns from South Africa and becomes known as the 'Mahatma' (Great Soul). The end of the war sees a new stirring of nationalist fervour.

1919
General Dyer fires on a nationalist protest in Amritsar, killing 379 and injuring over 1,200.

1920s
National movement gathers strength; Gandhi propounds the theory of *satyagraha* (non-violent non-cooperation); all Nationalist leaders spend time in prison. In 1927 Congress demands full independence.

February, 1931
Sir Edwin Lutyens' planned city of New Delhi is officially inaugurated.

1932
Congress splits after Gandhi demands full political rights for the Harijans (untouchables).

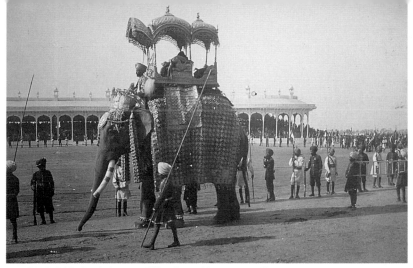

The 1911 Delhi Durbar, in honour of King George V, was a magnificent affair

1935–39

The Government of India Act aims to set up a federation of autonomous states with Dominion status. The first state elections in 1937 lead to huge Congress majority.

1939–45

India is involved in World War II without consultation, and Dominion status is put on hold. Extremist leader, Subhas Chandra Bose allies with the Nazis. In 1940 the Muslim League demands a separate Muslim state. In 1942 Gandhi and Jawaharlal Nehru lead a 'Quit India' campaign, during which 1,000 people are killed and 60,000 arrested.

1947

UK Labour Government accepts the idea of independence. A partition plan by Viceroy Lord Louis Mountbatten is accepted. On 15 August, India gains independence with Nehru as first Prime Minister of India. Fighting breaks out between Muslims, Sikhs and Hindus as up to 12 million people trek north to Pakistan or south to India. By the end, anything from half to one million people are dead.

January 1948

Gandhi is killed by a Hindu extremist.

1949

In exchange for a privy purse and the retention of titles, the Maharajahs give up their power and lands and join the Union. The 23 principalities later become Rajasthan (land of the Rajas).

1965

India fights Pakistan over land disputes.

1970

Indira Gandhi abolishes the privy purse and the royal titles.

1971

Pakistan is split; creation of Bangladesh. Pakistani refugees flee into Rajasthan.

1984

Indira Gandhi (prime minister 1966–77 and 1980–4) is assassinated by members of her Sikh bodyguard.

1991

Rajiv Gandhi, son of Indira, is killed by Tamil extremists in Madras.

Culture

*T*he cities may have just a large enough sprinkling of Western-style liberalism to confuse the visitor, but most of India lives by rules stretching back thousands of years. Whatever their beliefs, religion (see pages 18–21) is more than a faith to all Indians; it is an inextricable part of the fabric of society.

Caste

With Hinduism comes a rigid caste system (see page 138) that has also spread, in a less virulent form, to India's other religions. Your caste has nothing to do with your financial standing or your education. The Brahmin peasant has a higher social standing than the Dalit (untouchable) doctor. A few daring souls may marry out of caste and the Dalits do now have some constitutional rights, but few have any real chance of hauling themselves on to even the lowest rung of the social ladder. Many don't even try – they believe it is their *karma* (fate) and hope for a better deal in the next life.

Lifestyle

Most Indian men are hardworking, although the work is done at their own pace and in their own time. By preference, they love nothing more than to talk, whether to gossip, thrash out political theory or satisfy their own curiosity, and spend their leisure time hanging around in cafés or shady street corners with the other men. The educated are great readers and thinkers. Few men would ever dream of lifting a hand to help around the house.

Some women do have careers and a degree of freedom. Many more live desperately constricted lives, rarely stirring outside the home and fields. Most marriages are still arranged, often between children barely into their teens, and a dowry system flourishes.

Rajasthan

Rajasthan, for all its glories, is deeply reactionary, poverty-stricken, poorly educated and backward-looking. There are 72 Rajput sub-castes, 108 types of Brahmin, 52 castes of traders (including the Jains) and 308 lower castes.

The Rajputs (see pages 92–3) still

Young girls in festive finery on their way to make a temple offering

Indian men love to read and chat above all else

reign supreme. There is money, among the Rajputs and the Jains, but most people scratch a living along the poverty line. Conversely, some may seem poor when you see their humble village home, but the women are draped in heavy silver jewellery and the little boy is guarding a herd of 30 camels. Among the former nomads, wealth is mobile, portable or on the hoof.

As a whole, the Rajasthanis are a beautiful people, their classic features adorned by bright colours and rich ornamentation. The men are often peacocks, all too aware of their appearance, from the colour and ornate pattern of the turban, which proclaims the caste, occupation and home area of the wearer, to the dashing curl of the moustache.

The women, too, look gorgeous but if they have a tough life elsewhere, in Rajasthan it can be brutal. As in medieval Europe, the chivalric Rajput warriors swore to love and protect their fragile female flowers. One way to do this was by adopting the Muslim custom of purdah. In high society, this left the women with nothing to do; as the custom trickled downwards, women were almost entirely cut off from the outside world even while they worked like galley slaves, bringing up huge quantities of children, doing all the cooking and cleaning, and most of the farming – growing old before their time. Little has changed. Because the dowry must be repaid if the woman is divorced, all too many are victims of accidents, and there are still even cases of *sati* (the ritual burning of a wife on her husband's funeral pyre), even though it has long been illegal. One young man described it as sacred and then added that the women wanted it, because their lives as widows would be so much worse!

Religion

HINDUISM

To be Hindu is not just to follow a religion but also describes your race, way of life and whole being. There is no way to become, or stop being a Hindu and the religion, which arrived in India in the 2nd millennium BC with the Aryan people, is flexible enough to incorporate almost any beliefs.

As a Hindu, you live in a cycle of endless reincarnation (*samsara*), your deeds in this life determining your fate (*karma*) in the next. There are four aims: to live life properly and acquire merit (*dharma*), make money (*artha*), satisfy desire (*kama*) and to reach *moksha*, the end of the cycle of rebirth, and merge with **Bhagvan**, the soul of the universe. There are three essential duties, worship (*puja*), the cremation of the dead, and adherence to the caste system (see page 138).

There are rituals for every occasion, thousands of festivals (see pages 158–9) and pilgrimages are as popular as package tours. However, normal worship is essentially private. People pop into the temple in passing to make an offering of flowers or fruit and money, and receive a blessing. Every household has a shrine, tended by the women. Even the morning wash is a prayer, as spiritual and physical purity are regarded as one.

The Gods

There is a huge pantheon of gods, goddesses, minor spirits and demons. However, most are actually different aspects or incarnations of the same few. At the top of the tree are Brahma (the

Pilgrims make *puja* (worship) before the great bull, Nandi, vehicle of Shiva

Creator), Shiva (the Destroyer), and Vishnu (the Preserver) – themselves probably different aspects of Bhagvan.

Although priests are called Brahmins, only one active temple to **Brahma** is left in India, at Pushkar, Rajasthan.

Vishnu is usually portrayed with a discus, conch shell, mace and lotus blossom. He rides the half-man, half-eagle **Garuda**. He has appeared nine times so far, when the earth was in great need. The most important incarnations are: the 7th, the hero **Rama**, whose epic adventures are told in the classical poem, the *Ramayana*; the 8th, the womanising **Krishna**, usually portrayed with a flute, a blue face, or with erotic statues; and the 9th, the **Buddha**, Prince Sidhartha Gautam, founder of Buddhism.

Shiva is worshipped under many names reflecting different aspects of his character. Above all, he is the god of procreation and his most common symbol is the phallic *lingam*. He is also shown with a third eye, sign of wisdom and power.

Of the goddesses, the most powerful is **Parvati**, wife of Shiva and sister of Vishnu, who is worshipped as the mother goddess and as the terrifying **Durga** and **Kali**, goddess of destruction. **Lakshmi**, wife of Vishnu, is the goddess of wealth and good fortune, with several impressive temples built by grateful millionaires.

Other gods are the elephant-headed **Ganesh**, god of wisdom and prosperity, and the monkey god, **Hanuman**, who helped Rama on his quest.

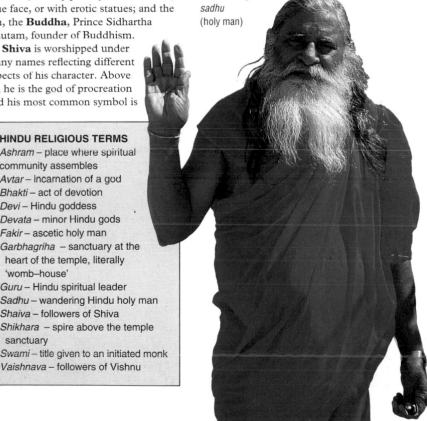

A wandering *sadhu* (holy man)

HINDU RELIGIOUS TERMS
Ashram – place where spiritual community assembles
Avtar – incarnation of a god
Bhakti – act of devotion
Devi – Hindu goddess
Devata – minor Hindu gods
Fakir – ascetic holy man
Garbhagriha – sanctuary at the heart of the temple, literally 'womb–house'
Guru – Hindu spiritual leader
Sadhu – wandering Hindu holy man
Shaiva – followers of Shiva
Shikhara – spire above the temple sanctuary
Swami – title given to an initiated monk
Vaishnava – followers of Vishnu

Above: Muslim at prayer, Jama Masjid, Delhi
Right: Qur'anic inscriptions adorn many
mosques

ISLAM

Islam was founded in Mecca (now Saudi
Arabia) by the Prophet Mohammed
(*c* AD570–632). In 622, he and his
followers were flung out and trekked
north to Medina. This event, the *hegira*,
marks the birth of the faith. The new
religion grew rapidly. By 628,
Mohammed had conquered Mecca. By
the early 8th century, Islam controlled
most of Arabia and was spreading west
into Europe and east towards India.
Conquest of Delhi was finally achieved in
1192. Today, there are over 100 million
Muslims in India.

The religion follows the teachings of
the Prophet, revealed to him in a series

ISLAMIC RELIGIOUS TERMS
Allah – God
Dargah – shrine or tomb of a Muslim
saint
Imam – Shi'ite holy man
Imambara – tomb of an Imam
Masjid – mosque (Jama Masjid
means Friday Mosque)
Mihrab – niche in a mosque pointing
the way to Mecca
Minbar – steps beside the mihrab
pointing the way to heaven
Muezzin – man who calls the faithful
to prayer
Minaret – tower from which the call to
prayer is broadcast
Qur'an (Koran) – the holy book of
Islam
Shi'ite – hard–line sect which broke
away soon after the death of
Mohammed, believing that the
religion should be led absolutely by
a direct descendent of the prophet.
Now ruled by a council of Ayatollahs.
Sunni – the main body of Islam,
which regards imams as teachers
and guides and accepts no absolute
authority but God. Most Indian
Muslims are Sunni.
Sufi – ascetic Muslim sect with mystic
beliefs

of divine revelations from the one God, Allah, and set down in the Qur'an. Islam means 'submission to God'. The Five Pillars of Islam (essential duties) include: prayer five times a day; the creed 'There is no God but God and Mohammed is the messenger of God'; the month-long fast of Ramadan; alms-giving; and if possible, the Haj – the journey to Mecca.

JAINISM

An off-shoot of Hinduism, the Jain religion was founded in the 6th century BC by Mahavira (literally 'great hero') Vardhamana Jnatputra, the son of a wealthy family, who became a wandering ascetic. It was originally purely monastic; a lay version (still considered inferior) wasn't conceived for another century. Mahavira said that true followers must renounce everything. After his death, there was a split between the *digambara* ('sky–clad') who believed this meant rejecting all clothes and the *shvetambaras* ('white-clad') who felt that a simple white robe could be allowed.

Jainism is basically atheistic, worshipping the 24 *tirthankars* as great teachers, not as gods. The universe is divided into four levels: the underworld, earth, celestial world and the *Siddha-loka* (paradise). Each living being has two parts, the impure *ajiva* (body) and the pure, self-contained *jiva* (soul). The aim is to detach yourself from the physical world through sacrifice, breaking the chains of the body to let the soul go free. It takes many lives.

Monks and nuns travel for about eight months of the year, gathering to study and meditate during the monsoon. They renounce all possessions and live celibate lives. As a final renunciation of the flesh, the old are sometimes allowed to starve themselves to death on the road to paradise.

Lay Jains must wait to become monks and women to be reborn as men before they can make real progress, but even they must worship daily and go on pilgrimage. They are strict vegetarians and can kill no living creature – not from pity but as a break with greed, materialism and aggression. In spite of that, the Jains are renowned traders, and the superb beauty of many Jain temples is the result of commercial profit. There are about 4 million Jains in India.

Jain monks lead an arduous life, based on total renunciation of worldly goods

Politics

*I*ndian politics are extraordinary. The country is fragmented and volatile, quickly aroused to protest and, often fatally, to riot. There have been campaigns of civil disobedience, internal terrorism and assassinations. There are frequent claims of corruption and electoral rigging. Yet the country remains firmly committed to democracy, there has never been any suggestion of a military coup, there is freedom of press and speech, and the judiciary is independent and often outspoken. The constitution is, on paper at least, one of the most liberal and idealistic in the world, although many aspects are widely ignored in favour of traditional custom or expediency. Most Indians are totally astonished when onlookers express fears that the country may rip itself to pieces.

The Constitution

India is a federal republic within the Commonwealth, with a written constitution that enshrines several high ideals, including universal suffrage, a ban on untouchability, equal rights for women and a declaration of human rights. There are two houses of parliament. The *Lok Sabha* (House of the People) has 542 members and represents the people as a whole, with 125 seats reserved for the Scheduled Castes and two nominated representatives of the Anglo-Indian population. The *Rajya Sabha* (Council of State) has 250 members, representing the Federal States. Each state then has its own legislative assembly or *Vidhan Sabha*. Central government controls defence, foreign affairs, currency, railways, post and ports. The states are responsible for education, agriculture, industry and the police. The Prime Minister, leader of the majority party, governs with the aid of a cabinet. The figurehead president has the right to intervene only if central or state government has collapsed.

Congress and the Nehru Dynasty

Since it was founded back in 1885, the Congress Party has been the over-whelmingly dominant force in the country's politics, remaining in power for all but seven years since 1947. For most of that time it has been led by a member of the Nehru family. In the 1920s Motilal Nehru was co-author of a first draft constitution. In 1947 his son, Jawaharlal, became the country's first

Prime Minister, ruling until his death in 1964. In 1966 his daughter, Indira Gandhi, took over, remaining in power for all but 3 years, until she was assassinated in 1984. Within hours, her son, Rajiv had been sworn in, remaining in office until 1989. In 1991 he was killed by Tamil separatists. In the ensuing upheaval, Congress tried to persuade Rajiv's apolitical, European wife to stand; she refused and the dynasty came to an end. Congress is still in power, however, under the current leadership of P V Narasimha Rao, and there are persistent rumours that Priyanka Gandhi, Indira's young granddaughter, is being groomed to take centre stage.

The BJP

The rapidly growing Bharatiya Janata Party looks set to be the first real threat to Congress – and the stability of India. Right-wing, reactionary and committed to Hindu fundamentalism, the BJP promises to turn India into a religious state, ruled by Hindu law. Whipping up grassroots support and mob hysteria, it has been involved in many acts of aggression, such as the destruction of the mosque in Ayodhya. Electoral success in 1991 led Congress to invoke President's Rule in five north Indian states, including Rajasthan, and order new elections, held in November 1993. Congress claimed back very narrow majorities in most cases, but the BJP won a landslide victory in Delhi. Supporters claim that the rhetoric will be toned down if the party wins nationally; non-Hindus and members of the Scheduled Castes are all terrified. It is probable, however, that India's genius for political stability will yet again prevail, against all odds.

Congress leaders, including Pandit Nehru (centre) meet at a conference, 1947

GANDHI

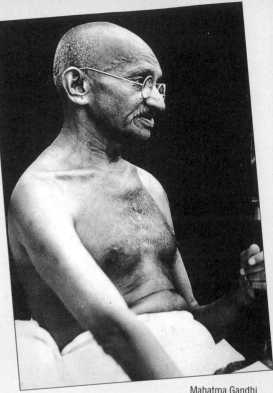

Mahatma Gandhi
(the Great Soul), 1869–1948

Born in 1869, son of the hereditary Prime Minister of Kathiawar, Gujarat, Mohandas Karamchand Gandhi married Kastur Ba as a child before studying as a barrister in London. A practising lawyer, his political career began in South Africa when he was thrown out of a whites-only train carriage.

Returning to India as a hero in 1915, he was given the name Mahatma (Great Soul) by India's Nobel Prize-winning poet, Rabindranath Tagore. He quickly became a leader of the nationalist move-ment, espousing a philosophy of non-violent non-cooperation, *satyagraha*, based on a belief in love as a powerful force for change.

In 1920 he launched the first national campaign of civil disobedience. In 1921 he abandoned Western dress and adopted the plain white homespun *dhoti*, both as a protest against foreign cloth imports and in solidarity with the untouchables, whom he renamed the Harijan (Children of God). His dream was to destroy the caste system and make independent India a truly classless society. In 1930 he led a 200-mile march to the sea to make salt and break the government monopoly of this industry. In 1942, he launched the 'Quit India' campaign. Between negotiations with the government, he spent a number of years in jail and embarked on several hunger strikes as a way of breaking political deadlock.

Gandhi was opposed to the Partition of India and in 1947 once again went on hunger strike, to try and stop the resulting massacre. That he succeeded shows his immense stature among all Indians, but there was a tragic sting. Because of this so-called support for Muslims, he was assassinated by a Hindu extremist in his Delhi garden on 30 January 1948. A totally extraordinary man, as politician, philosopher and social crusader, he is still venerated in India and across the world.

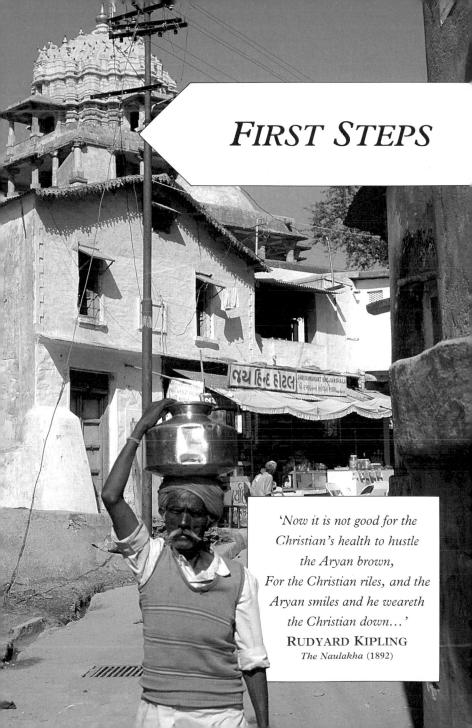

FIRST STEPS

'Now it is not good for the
Christian's health to hustle
the Aryan brown,
For the Christian riles, and the
Aryan smiles and he weareth
the Christian down...'
RUDYARD KIPLING
The Naulakha (1892)

Urban transport – fleets of creaking cycle- and growling auto-rickshaws prowl Delhi

GETTING AROUND

The roads may seem like a zoo but very few Indians have private cars or even motor-scooters, and as a result the country has one of the most efficient and affordable public transport systems in the world.

Cars

It is rarely worth hiring a car in the main cities as there are numerous taxis, all of which are happy to set a reasonable rate for the full day. Small towns have few if any taxis and you may have to arrange for one from the nearest city or do a deal with a local to hire his private car for the day. For out of town touring by car, all the international car hire companies have offices in the major cities. They will probably insist on you having a driver, but wages are cheap and you save the cost of insurance, so it can be financially worthwhile as well as a psychological godsend. Consider going one stage further, book through a travel agent and use a driver/guide who will speak better English, act as a personal courier and iron out any problems you face *en route*. It costs little more.

Outboards, horses and pedal power

Auto-rickshaws, tricycles with an outboard motor and a lid, are the mainstay of urban transport in India, zipping through the traffic at exhaust pipe level. Some people loath them, others become addicted. Some towns also have slightly larger autos which take up to 10 people and act as shared taxis. Cycle rickshaws are less common these days but do still exist. Try one for the experience but they are really only suitable for short distances and they can be very alarming in heavy traffic. In a very few country towns you will meet tongas, drawn by ageing skeletal nags.

Buses

There are plenty of buses, almost all very uncomfortable and overcrowded. The real killers are the luxury long-distance coaches which come with lace curtains, videos and Hindi pop music. Before you book consider that some inter-city

FARE PRICE

Taxis and autos all have meters, they are all meant to work and almost none of them do. If they do and the driver is actually prepared to use them, don't expect to pay what is actually on the dial. Meters can never be upgraded fast enough to keep up with inflation, so the municipality hands out cards with the new prices on, or sets a rate – meter plus 25 per cent or similar. Most of the time, you must set a price before you get in, and this involves some serious haggling. Ask someone friendly roughly how long your journey is and what the fare should be before you start. If you are in the wrong place, for example the gateway of a five-star hotel or the front of the railway station, expect the first price to be several times higher than normal. As a rule of thumb elsewhere, look to drop the price by half to two-thirds. If you are doing a lot of running around, it is well worth hiring someone for a half or whole day. You have transport on tap, and save yourself enormous amounts of aggravation.

Above: country buses are well used, usually carrying three times the legal number of passengers. Below: four-footed transport is still alive and kicking

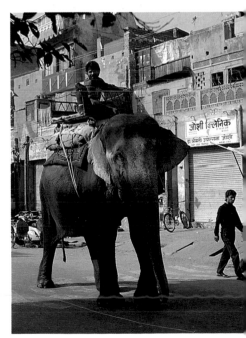

journeys last over 10 hours. Every town has a central bus station. They are usually chaotic, with no recognisable system of platforms or bays. Just keep asking everyone you meet if you are in the right place; sooner or later, you will be. Local services can be harder to find as there is never a timetable or list of routes. However, autos are cheap enough to justify using them.

For Planes, see page 178; for trains, see pages 28–9.

Licensed porters are recognisable by their usually faded red jackets and turbans

Waterloo) are teeming with life from beggars to businessmen, while children, cows and pigs roam freely.

Indrail Passes

Available only abroad or in selected major railway stations, rail passes are usually more expensive than booking individual tickets, but you will get preferential treatment and save a lot of time and hassle. The recommended first-class pass includes IIAC (air-conditioned second class, but better than fan-cooled first class). There are one- to 90-day versions, the most useful being 7 days (US$135), 15 days (US$165), 21 days (US$200) and 30 days (US$250). Sleepers for night travel are free.

Choosing Your Train

Outlying places may have only one or two trains a day. Other routes have a great many but the travelling time can vary enormously (for example from 2 hours to 4½ hours between Delhi and Agra), dependent on the type of train. Mail trains and passenger trains are slowest, express trains relatively slow and superfast express really are fast. All services have numbers and names. Many of the most convenient are overnight or leave at the crack of dawn.

Reservations

All major stations have a tourist booking office or window. For overnight journeys, reserve a berth as far ahead as possible, even if you have a pass. Fill in a form with the name and number of the train and your personal details. If you get stuck on a stand-by list, ask about the tourist quota – a few places may have been held back.

INDIAN RAILWAYS

Founded in 1853, one of the earliest and busiest networks in the world (and the world's largest employer, with over 1.8 million employees), Indian Railways carries over 4,500 million passengers a year. A recent massive upgrade programme has been converting all the tracks in Rajasthan to broad gauge, bringing in fast, modern capabilities. A sad by-product has been the virtual demise of steam. Nevertheless, train travel is an experience not to be missed. The very few superfast, air-conditioned, first-class carriages are similar to European second class. Normal first class is much scruffier, while second class has hard benches and heaving heaps of bodies. The extraordinarily grand stations (imperial Indian, by way of

The Palace on Wheels
The ultimate train trip, this luxury seven-day train cruise whistles round Rajasthan for US$200 per person per day. The original train used vintage carriages; the new version is an excellent replica with air-conditioning and proper plumbing.

Further Information
SD Enterprises Ltd, 103 Wembley Park Drive, Wembley, Middx HA9 8HG (tel: 0181–903 3411; fax: 0181–903 0392). Indian Railways agents.
Hariworld Travels Inc., 30 Rockefeller Plaza, Shop 21, North Mezzanine, New York, NY 10112 (tel: 212–957 3000; fax: 212–495 2383). Indian Railways agents.
International Tourist Bureau, New Delhi Station, Chelmsford Road, New Delhi (tel: 373 4164).
Palace on Wheels, RTDC Central Reservation Offices (see page 189).
The bi-monthly *Thomas Cook Overseas Timetable* gives details of many rail, bus and shipping services worldwide,

Station soft drinks stall

including India. Available in the UK from some stations, any branch of Thomas Cook or by phoning 01733–268 943. In the USA, contact the Forsyth Travel Library Inc., 9154 West 57th St (PO Box 2975), Shawnee Mission, Kansas 66201–1375; tel: (800) 367 7982 (toll-free); fax: (913) 384 3553.

One of India's last few steam engines

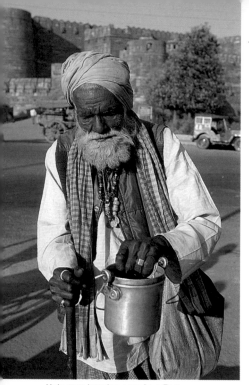

Holy man begging near Agra Fort

LIVING WITH INDIA

Culture Shock

India is hot, dirty and disease-ridden, with some of the most desperate poverty in the world. The bureaucracy is totally impassable. Nothing is ever simple and there is no privacy or peace. Curious crowds stare and giggle. Most of them want a piece of you, in conversation or cash. You can hide briefly inside the Westernised hotels, but that just means you never acclimatise, and are shocked anew each time you step outdoors.

Don't expect to have a relaxing holiday. Accept that you will spend much of your time in a state of bewildered chaos, will probably only understand what you experienced in about six months, and will arrive home far more

tired than when you left. Treat the queues, the crowds and the flies as part of the adventure and every so often, treat your sanity to a little luxury – a hot bath, a swim or a gin-and-tonic.

Baksheesh and Beggars

Baksheesh can be a tip, a donation to a beggar, a little something to smooth the path, or something expected of you, as a rich foreigner, for no reason at all. It is a word you will grow to hate. Once you have dealt with would-be guides, drivers, salesmen, and everyone else, India has enough beggars to populate some countries, all desperately pitiable. You cannot give to them all and should not give to some. Many are genuinely needy, but there are organised begging rings and children do get mutilated to push up their price with bleeding-heart foreigners. You will also be swamped if you hand out cash. You would do better to give a decent donation to a suitable charity.

Etiquette

Always greet people politely, with a smile. Men can shake hands but women should fold their hands (as in prayer). Men and women never touch in public, and this extends to your own husband/wife. Only Westernised men will shake hands with a woman. Never use your left hand for eating or for giving anything to someone else (the left hand is kept for ablutions).

Religious Etiquette

Although there are many religions and sects, the basic rules of etiquette in places of worship are the same. Always dress modestly – no shorts and no bare shoulders. Always take off your shoes. The shoeminder by the door will expect a tip of one or two rupees. Never take leather into a Jain temple. A few temples may bar non-Hindus from the inner sanctum, but most will encourage you to take part in any celebration and show you the ropes. Try to avoid mosques at Friday lunch time, but you will be welcome at other times.

Women Travellers

The Indians may find you bizarre, but travelling on your own is not a problem. You will get requests for everything from a quick fling to marriage, but they are usually polite and a firm 'no' works wonders. Personal questions stem from curiosity and they are astonished if you seem offended. Dress conservatively; many women in Rajasthan still live in purdah, and if you show too much flesh, you become fair game. Most Indian women do not drink or smoke.

Right: shoes left by the temple door
Below: whole families clamour for *baksheesh*

Indian tourists are also very keen photographers

PHOTOGRAPHY

The most visually stunning region of the most photogenic country in the world, Rajasthan positively aches to be photographed, while the Taj Mahal, in neighbouring Uttar Pradesh, must be one of the most photographed buildings on the planet. In other words, take far more film than you would ever expect to want and you will probably still end up needing more. It is possible to buy film in most tourist areas, but the range on offer is limited and you should always check the sell-by date. The light is good, if too harsh at midday, so take mainly slow film, with some faster for interiors and evenings.

You are allowed to take photos inside many monuments, museums and temples, but you will usually need to buy an additional photo ticket or pay a donation to a nearby monk (who will also pose, if the price is right). If you use a tripod, you will probably be classified as professional and the cost goes up dramatically. Video cameras are a real nuisance, as they have to be declared on entry, they are forbidden in many places and in others the price for using them is very high. Photography of any military installation (including bridges) or soldiers is forbidden. People usually turn a blind eye at the stations, otherwise just ask the superintendent for permission or apply for a permit from The Director of Public Relations, Railway Board, Rail Bhuwan, New Delhi 110 001.

Some beggars, snake charmers and opportunists will ask for money; set a rate before you start clicking. However, most Indians, apart from women in purdah, love being photographed and huge crowds will line up as soon as they spot the camera. You will also find Indian tourists asking to take pictures of you – it seems only fair to let them!

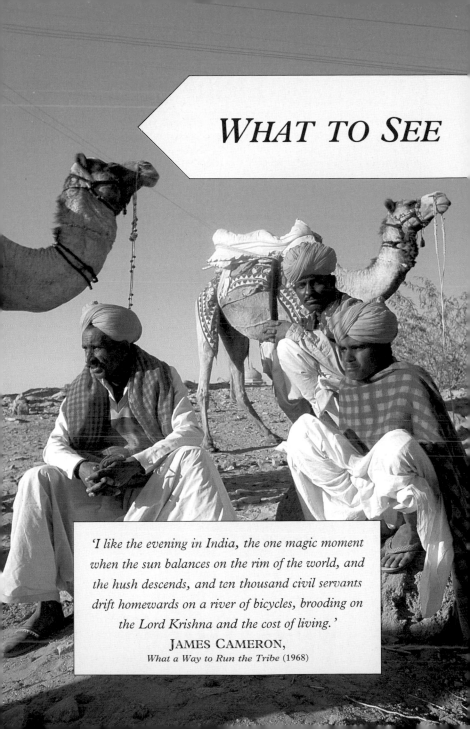

WHAT TO SEE

'I like the evening in India, the one magic moment
when the sun balances on the rim of the world, and
the hush descends, and ten thousand civil servants
drift homewards on a river of bicycles, brooding on
the Lord Krishna and the cost of living.'
JAMES CAMERON,
What a Way to Run the Tribe (1968)

Delhi

*D*elhi has a pedigree stretching back at least 4,500 years, with around 20,000 known ruins and 1,300 listed monuments. Moreover, for most of its life, it has been an imperial capital, and the home of kings. Today, it is the capital of a united India and the third largest city on the subcontinent, with a growing population of around 9 million.

A huge north–south sprawl along the banks of the Yamuna River, the city has two distinct and very different centres. To the south are the wide tree-lined boulevards and colonnaded mansions of British-built New Delhi, the official seat of government. Just to the north, Moghul Old Delhi is an overcrowded frenzy of narrow winding streets and alleys. Beyond in every direction spread suburbs and housing colonies, blocks of flats, and carefully away from the centre, an oozing mass of shanty towns and slums.

When most people arrive, they are disappointed by how tatty the city centre seems. A few weeks later, the lucky ones look behind the peeling paint and faded posters and suddenly see a different city glowing with wealth and modernity – by Indian standards. Both impressions are right. Like the rest of India, Delhi has a multiple personality. It isn't instantly and obviously beautiful: you will see desperate poverty; the constant press of people can be irritating; and the city is shadowed by a pall of pollution. Yet given time, you will begin to feel the sheer weight of history, the grace and good nature, and the constant buzz of excitement that make this one of the great cities of the world.

> *'[Delhi] is the most uncertain-minded of cities in the world. It is like a fidgety girl who will first sit here, and there, then somewhere else, and fifty square miles of ground and twenty thousand ruins tell where it has rested.'*
> JOHN FOSTER FRASER,
> *Round the World on a Wheel* (1899)

Connaught Place, at the centre of New Delhi

DELHI CITY

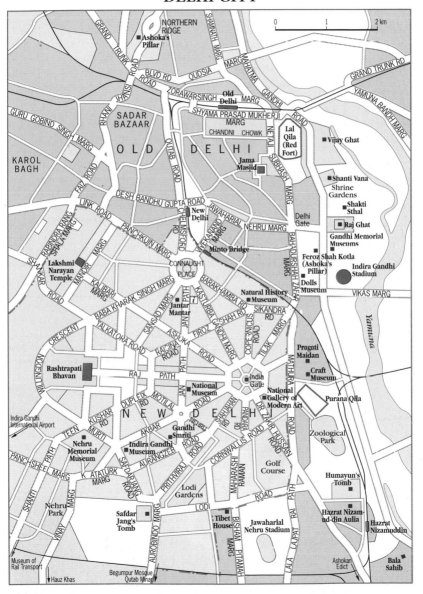

major quarrel with the Tughluq king, Ghiyas-ud-Din, over who got to use some workmen, he prophesied that the new city of Tughluqabad would become a home for sheep and that the king wouldn't live to see Delhi again. Both prophesies came true. The existing domed tomb was a replacement built in 1526. Numerous dignitaries are buried near by. Qawwali prayers (mystical poems) are sung at about 7pm each evening and all night during the twice-yearly Urs fairs.
Opposite Humayun's tomb, off Mathura Road (no telephone). Open access.

HUMAYUN'S TOMB

The Emperor Humayun died in 1556, tripping down the stairs of the Purana

Left: the extraordinary geometry of the Jantar Mantar. Below: the onion domes of the Jama Masjid, Old Delhi

BAHA'I HOUSE OF WORSHIP

This enormous lotus blossom of white concrete and marble was completed in 1986. Its nine sides and nine reflective pools symbolise comprehensiveness, oneness and unity, while the lotus is a traditional Indian symbol of purity and holiness. There are around 28,000 Baha'i communities in India, dedicated to promoting worldwide peace, harmony and unity.
Bahapur, Kalkaji, South Delhi (tel: 644 4029). Open: April to September, Tuesday to Sunday, 9am–7pm; October to March, 9.30am–5.30pm. Admission free.

CONNAUGHT PLACE, see page 47.

HAZRAT NIZAM-UD-DIN AULIA

One of the holiest Islamic sites in India, this is the *dargah* of a Sufi saint, Nizam-ud-Din Chishti (1236–1325). During a

Qila on his way to prayers. His magnificent mausoleum, completed in 1573 by his senior widow, Bega Begam, is the first of the great Moghul buildings in India, a huge octagonal building of red sandstone, inlaid with white and black marble, resting upon an arcaded plinth and topped by a bulbous 42.5m-high double dome. Set four square in formal walled gardens divided by water channels (*char bagh* design), it created the pattern followed by generations of classic Islamic garden tombs, including the Taj Mahal. Most of the tombs in the grounds are royal, but the most elaborate belong to the king's barber and bangle-maker.
Off Mathura Road, southeast Delhi, near Nizam-ud-din Station (no telephone). Open: sunrise to sunset. Admission charge.

INDIA GATE, see page 46.

JAMA MASJID (Friday Mosque)
Built between 1650 and 1656 by Emperor Shah Jahan, this is the largest and most splendid mosque in India, capable of holding 25,000 people. Constructed from red sandstone, marble and black onyx, it has three gates, four towers, two minarets, three black-and-white striped domes and three pulpits so that three *imams* can pray simultaneously to the immense crowds. Perched on a small hill and high plinth, it was originally and aptly named the Masjid-i-Jahan Nama (Mosque with a View of the World). A small museum in the cloisters holds holy relics, including a hair from Mohammed's beard, his sandals and footprint set in stone.
Opposite the Red Fort, Netaji Subhash Marg (tel: 326 8344). Open: daily, sunrise to 12.20pm; 1.45pm until 5 minutes before

afternoon prayer call; after prayers until 20 minutes before sunset. Admission free, but photo charge.

JANTAR MANTAR
One of five observatories built by Jaipur's astronomer king, Jai Singh II, in 1724, this may look like a playground but is in fact a complex system for measuring time (accurate to half a second), seasons, the movements of the moon and even the signs of the zodiac. (See also page 97.)
Sansad Marg (no telephone). Open: daily, sunrise to sunset. Admission charge.

LAKSHMI NARAYAN TEMPLE
A large, somewhat gaudy temple, built in 1938 by the industrialist Birla family and dedicated to the goddess of wealth. An example of modern Hinduism in action.
Mandir Marg (tel: 343 637). Open access.

The modern Lakshmi Narayan Temple is a monument to capitalism and the goddess of wealth

Lal Qila
(Red Fort)

*W*hen Shah Jahan moved his capital to Delhi, he built a magnificent palace, decorated it with marble and precious stones, tapestries and carpets, created formal gardens set with gushing fountains and called it the *Qila-e-Mubarak* (Fortunate Citadel). Work began in 1638, took nearly 10 years and cost almost Rs 90 million. Its current prosaic title is something of a let down, matched by its sorry state after earthquakes (1719), invasion by the Persian king, Nadir Shah (1739), attacks by Marathas and Jats (1759) and a fire set by Gulam Qader (1798). After the 1857 Mutiny, the last Moghul emperor, Bahadur Shah II, was tried here, some two-thirds of its buildings were demolished to make way for army barracks (on the left, by the water tower) and much of the palace's remaining finery was stripped out by the British. At midnight on 14 August 1947, the new flag was raised here to mark Indian independence.

The Walls

The roughly octagonal blood-red sandstone walls measure 2.4km round, 18 to 33m high and are surrounded by a 9m-deep moat, fed by the Yamuna River. Of the five gates, only the **Lahore Gate** remains in use, its triumphal effect blocked by a massive barbican built by Emperor Aurangzeb. Inside, the **Chatta Chowk** (covered market) was built to sell luxury goods to the courtiers.

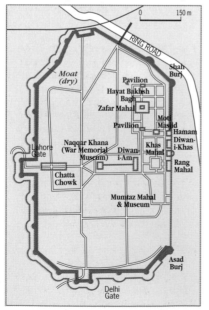

Naubat or Naqqar Khana (Drum House)

Just inside the entrance, this three-storey building was used to play music and fanfares, and as the visitors' elephant park. Two emperors, Jahandar Shah (1712–13) and Farrukhsiyar (1713–19) were murdered here. The upper storeys house a small **War Memorial Museum**.

Diwan-i-Am

Directly ahead, the emperor would hold court each morning in the **Hall of Public Audience,** his throne perched on the massive platform, with the Wazir (Prime Minister) sitting on the bench in front. Curtains and carpets decorated the pavilion, which at that time would have been plastered and gilded. Behind the

The Lahore Gate is now the only entrance to Shah Jahan's massive Red Fort

throne is an intricate marble panel, created by the Florentine jeweller, Austin de Bordeaux.

Private Quarters

The inner palace consists of a string of small pavilions along the river wall. On the far left, the delicately carved marble **Moti Masjid** (Pearl Mosque) was built by Aurangzeb in 1659. A canopy shaded the courtyard in which a fountain ran hot and cold water. Behind it is the **Hamam**, or Royal Bath House. To the right of this, the **Diwan-i-Khas** (Hall of Private Audience) was the real centre of government and home of the Peacock Throne of solid gold decorated with jewelled peacocks, stolen by Nadir Shah and taken to Tehran.

At the centre of the complex, the **Khas Mahal** (Private Palace) was the emperor's own quarters. The emperor would wave to his subjects from the balcony behind this building every morning and evening. The harem buildings began with the **Rang Mahal** (known as the House of Colour or House of Mirrors for its once brilliant decoration). The whole area was cooled by underfloor streams, pools and fountains called the **Nahr-i-Bihist** (Stream of Paradise). On the far right, the marble **Mumtaz Mahal** now houses the **Museum of Archaeology**.

Off Nataji Subhash Marg, Old Delhi (tel: 326 7961/327 3703). Open: daily, 9am–5pm; museums, 10am–5pm (closed Friday). Admission charge (free on Friday). Son-et-lumière, see page 156.

CITY STREETS

There is a fight for supremacy on the road involving one brightly painted lorry belching black smoke, three battered buses, with people clinging to windows and bumpers like barnacles, numerous snarling black and yellow auto-rickshaws, a camel-cart laden with fridges, a couple of shiny Ambassador cars and a family of five on a motor-scooter. The few spaces between are taken up by a positive regiment of young men on elderly black bicycles, and coming up from behind is an elephant. The lorry sports a sign that says 'Horn, please' – everybody else is only too eager to oblige and the noise level is fantastic. Slap bang in the middle of the road, several creamy-white cows with painted horns have sat down to chew the cud and watch the traffic swirl around them.

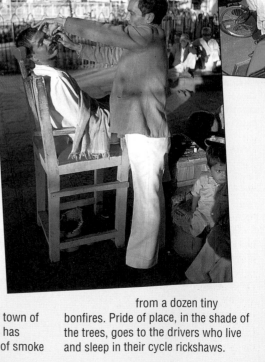

Half-a-dozen ragged children, cripples and lepers dodge through the mayhem, thrusting grubby hands into any open window. 'Rupee, just one rupee, my mother is ill, my father is ill…' On a tiny patch of open ground a shanty town of cardboard and corrugated iron has sprung up, puffing little gasps of smoke from a dozen tiny bonfires. Pride of place, in the shade of the trees, goes to the drivers who live and sleep in their cycle rickshaws.

Beside them, a barber has set up shop with a chair, a pair of scissors and a bucket of water, and an old woman with a hand cart is selling peeled cucumbers and roast corn.

Near by, a row of narrow, open-fronted shops is doing brisk business in anything from saucepans to Pepsi, blankets to statues of Ganesh. The older men sit cross-legged and calm, while milling crowds of young men in shiny nylon shirts and plastic thongs hang around waiting for something to happen. You, the hapless visitor, are not only a source of revenue, but also the entertainment.

India's streets are a whole world in themselves; people live, sleep, wash, eat, shop, chat and run their businesses in a haze of carbon monoxide and an ear-splitting cacophony of noise

MUSEUMS

CRAFT MUSEUM

A not-to-be-missed collection of crafts from across India, from toys to shrines, roof tiles to fishing traps, jewellery to puppets. Highlights include textiles, a reconstructed *haveli* and the Keralan Bhuta wood carvings. Outside, crafts demonstrators squat among reconstructed village houses.
Pragati Maidan, Bhairon Road (tel: 331 7641). Open: Tuesday to Sunday, 10am–5pm. Admission free.

GANDHI MEMORIAL MUSEUMS

These three museums celebrate the Mahatma (see page 24). The **Gandhi Darshan** displays his life, work and philosophy in photographs and paintings. The **Gandhi Smarak Sangrahalaya** is

> ### MINOR MUSEUMS
> For a full list of other museums, see *Delhi Diary*. Among the more interesting are:
> **Air Force Museum**, *Palam Marg, by Safdar Jung Airport.*
> **National Philatelic Museum** (see page 47)
> **National Science Centre Museum**, *Pragati Maidan.*
> **Natural History Museum** (see page 47)
> **Tibet House Museum**, *1 Institutional Area, Lodi Road.*

a more intimate collection of personal possessions. The colonial-style **Gandhi Smriti** was Gandhi's Delhi base. He was assassinated here in 1948. Inside is a fascinating display on his life; outside, a memorial stands in beautiful gardens.
Gandhi Darshan and Gandhi Smarak Sangrahalaya (closed Thursday) are both opposite Raj Ghat (tel: 331 1495/331 0168). Open: Tuesday to Sunday, 9.30am–5.30pm. A film in English is shown daily at 5pm. Admission free. Gandhi Smriti, 5 Tees January Marg (tel: 301 2843). Open: Tuesday to Sunday, 9am–5.30pm. Admission charge.

INDIRA GANDHI MUSEUM

This simple house was home to Indira and Rajiv Gandhi, with numerous photographs, newspaper reports and awards made to the mother and son prime ministers. The collection includes saris worn by Indira for her wedding and at her death, shot by members of her own guard in the grounds in 1984 (a memorial marks the spot), and the

Memorial statue to Mahatma Gandhi

Sculpture garden at the Museum of Modern Art

trainers Rajiv was wearing when he was assassinated by a bomb in Madras in 1991.

1 Safdarjang Road (tel: 301 0094). Open: Tuesday to Sunday, 9.30am–5pm. Admission free.

MUSEUM OF RAIL TRANSPORT

Contained within this museum is everything you would ever want to know about Indian railways, with photographs, models, 42 carefully preserved vintage locomotives, including the *Fairy Queen*, the oldest working engine in the world (built in 1855), 26 carriages, one used by the Prince of Wales, and a mini-train for children. Look for the elephant that tangled with a train (and nearly won) and the complaint from a man caught with his *dhoti* down.

Chanakyapuri (tel: 601 816). Open: October to March, Tuesday to Sunday, 9.30am–5pm; April to September, 9.30am–7pm; closed for lunch 1pm–1.30pm. Admission plus photo charge. A film (English) is shown at 11am and 3pm.

NATIONAL GALLERY OF MODERN ART

Little in this fine collection of mainly post-1930s Indian art, housed in the former palace of the Maharajah of Jaipur, harks back to classical style, treating Indian subjects with rare freedom of expression. Among the most interesting artists are Amrita Shergil, and the poet, Rabindranath Tagore. There is a sculpture garden in the grounds.

Jaipur House, India Gate (tel: 382 8359). Open: Tuesday to Sunday, 10am–5.30pm. Admission free.

NATIONAL MUSEUM, see page 44.

NEHRU MEMORIAL MUSEUM AND PLANETARIUM

Home of Jawaharlal Nehru (see pages 22–3), this mansion was built in 1930 for the British Commander-in-Chief. Inside, photos and newspapers tell the story of Nehru, from child to elder statesman. Several rooms are as he left them. A planetarium stands in the grounds.

Teen Murti Bhavan (tel: 301 6734). Open: Tuesday to Sunday, 9.30am–5pm (last entrance at 4.45pm). Planetarium open: 10am–4.45pm; performances in English at 11am and 3pm. Admission free.

SHANKAR'S INTERNATIONAL DOLLS MUSEUM

Over 6,000 dolls, collected by journalist and cartoonist, K Shankar Pillai. Among the finest are those clothed in traditional Indian regional costumes.

Bahadurshah Zafar Marg (tel: 331 6970). Open: Tuesday to Sunday, 10am–6pm. Admission charge.

NATIONAL MUSEUM

Allow a day to do real justice to India's national collection which includes a magnificent array of temple statuary, a wide range of costumes and textiles, miniature paintings, musical instruments, folk art, an archaeological collection (including Harappan and Gupta exhibits), a new heavily guarded jewellery gallery and much much more.
Janpath, just off Rajpath (tel: 301 9538). Open: Tuesday to Sunday, 10am–5pm. Regular film shows and guided tours. Admission and photo charge.

QUTAB MINAR COMPLEX

Site of the Rajput city of Dhilli/Lal Kot (see pages 50–1), this is better known for its magnificent Islamic buildings.

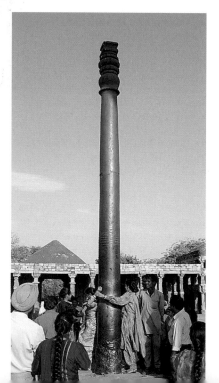

Qutab Minar

This superb, 72m high-tower (1193–1230) served a dual purpose, as a resplendent minaret and a very visible reminder of the area's new Islamic rulers. The original four-tier sandstone tower was built by Qutb-ud-Din-Aibak and Shamsu'd Din Iltutmish (1211–36). After the top storey was damaged by lightning in 1368, Feroz Shah Tughluq repaired it, adding two storeys of Rajasthani marble and sandstone. Today, the tower is five storeys high and slightly out of alignment after British repairs. With its adroit use of stone, preserved Qur'anic carvings and the imagination in each of the different tiers, it is one of the tallest and most beautiful minarets ever conceived. The **Ala'i Minar**, a second, bigger tower opposite, was begun by Ala-ud-Din Khalji (1296–1316) but was never completed.

Quwwat ul-Islam Masjid (Might of Islam Mosque)

Twenty-seven Hindu and Jain temples

Clasp the Iron Pillar and have your wish granted

THE IRON PILLAR

Brought here by one of the 10th- to 12th-century Tomar kings, the iron pillar is 7.2m high, weighs 6 tons, is made of 99.97 per cent pure iron, and has never rusted, to the bemusement of scientists. A Sanskrit inscription at the base shows it to be a 4th-century standard to the god Vishnu in memory of King Chandragupta II (375–413). If you can stretch round the pillar backwards to touch your hands together, your wishes will be granted – so they say.

were destroyed, but many of their columns and three sides of a temple courtyard were reused within this stunning mosque, the earliest extant in India (1193). The fourth side is a spectacular confection of seven types of stone, decorated with Qur'anic script. Standing in the courtyard is an **iron pillar** (see box on page 44). The mosque was extended on two occasions; first by Shamsu'd Din Iltutmish and then by Ala-ud-Din.

Other Sights

Behind the Qutab Minar is a purely Islamic monumental gateway, the **Ala'i Darwaza** (1311). Next to that is the small, attractive **tomb** of the early 16th-century Islamic saint, Imam Zamin. Behind the mosque are the remains of the **theological college** and the **tombs of Ala-ud-Din** and **Shamsu'd Din Iltutmish**. The latter is particularly beautiful, every inch of the exterior carved with Qur'anic script.

The Qutab Minar Complex is 15km south of Connaught Place off Aurobindo Marg. Open: sunrise to sunset. The tower is now closed to the public for safety. Admission charge.

RAJ GHAT

This peaceful park, along the old course of the Yamuna River, has become India's **Shrine Gardens**. At the southern end, a moving memorial marks the site of Mahatma Gandhi's cremation. Other memorials mark the cremation grounds of Jawaharlal Nehru (1964), Indira Gandhi (1984), Sanjay Gandhi (1980) and Rajiv Gandhi (1991).
South of the Red Fort. Open: April to September, daily, 5am–8pm; October to

The soaring Qutab Minar is a stunning monument to spiritual glory and earthly power

March, 5.30am–7.30pm. Admission free.

RAJPATH, see page 47.

SAFDAR JANG'S TOMB

Mirza Muqi Abu'l Mansur Khan (Safdar Jang being his title) was viceroy of Oudh and prime minister to Emperor Muhammed Shah. His mausoleum was built by his son in 1753–4 of highly decorated sandstone, with a central dome – the last of the classic Islamic garden tombs.
Safdarjang Road (no telephone). Open: sunrise to sunset. Admission and photo charge.

New Delhi

New Delhi was built between 1913 and 1930, a planned city of gracious boulevards and elegant colonial architecture, the work of Sir Edward Lutyens and Herbert Baker. Hire an auto-rickshaw or taxi. *Allow 2 hours minimum; a whole day if you plan to sightsee and shop.*

Start at India Gate.

1 INDIA GATE

This 42m triumphal arch is India's main war memorial, carved with the names of some 85,000 soldiers killed during World War I, on the North-West Frontier and during the Afghan Wars. Under the arch is an eternal flame, a memorial to soldiers who died during the 1971 Pakistan war and to the unknown soldier.

The cupola behind once housed a statue of King George V. Removed at independence, the promised replacement statue of Gandhi has never materialised.

In the surrounding circle of former princely palaces, Jaipur House is home to the National Gallery Of Modern Art (see page 43).

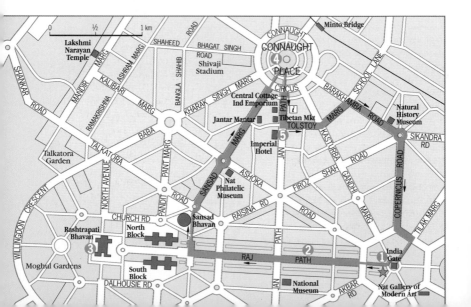

> '*Driving through the tremendous hexagonal parks and plazas that crisscross New Delhi, one has to admit that New Delhi is certainly crisscrossed with tremendous hexagonal parks and plazas.*'
> **S J PERELMAN,**
> *Westward Ho!* (1948)

Drive along Rajpath.

2 RAJPATH

This ceremonial boulevard really comes into its own for the annual Republic Day parade on 26 January. Sadly, the once splendid vista is now usually cloaked by a haze of pollution.

Continue up Rajpath. Halfway up, the road is intersected by Jan Path. Just to the left is the National Museum (see page 44).

3 RASHTRAPATI BHAVAN/ SECRETARIAT BUILDINGS

At the far end of the Rajpath, three vast imperial buildings squat on Raisina Hill. To either side, Herbert Baker's secretariat buildings house the Ministries of Finance and Foreign Affairs. At the back, Lutyens' magnificent Rashtrapati Bhavan, built as the Viceroy's house, is now the President's official residence. Larger than Versailles, with 340 rooms, it once had a staff of 2,000. The layout of the secretariat buildings, which blocks views of the classical mansion, caused a two-year feud between the two architects.

Turn right along Sansad Marg, past a large circular colonnaded building. This is the Sansad Bhavan (Houses of Parliament). At the junction with Ashoka Road is the important, but less than riveting, National Philatelic Museum. Further on is

Maharajah Jai Singh's outdoor observatory, the Jantar Mantar (see page 37).

4 CONNAUGHT PLACE

The heart of Lutyens' new city and the commercial centre of Delhi, this series of graceful colonnaded circles of shops and offices designed by Robert Tor Russell is in dire need of a coat of paint. At the centre is a scruffy roundabout.

Walk down the first section of Jan Path.

5 JAN PATH

The most famous of the radial roads, Jan Path is home to India's largest and best Central Cottage Industries Emporium and the roadside Tibetan Market. Opposite is the Government of India Tourist Office, and a little further on, the fine colonial Imperial Hotel has recently been given a new lease of life.

Turn on to Tolstoy Marg, then right on to Barakhamba Road, which leads back to India Gate via Copernicus Road, past the Natural History Museum.

National Philatelic Museum, *Dak Bhavan, Sansad Marg (tel: 371 0154/303 2451). Open: Monday to Friday, 9.30am–12.30pm and 2.30pm–4.30pm. Admission free.*
Natural History Museum, *FICCI Building, Barakhamba Rd (tel: 331 4849/331 4932). Open: Tuesday to Sunday, 10am–5pm. Admission charge.*
None of the state buildings are open to the public, although the Moghul-style garden of the Rashtrapati Bhavan is open in February and March.

Old Delhi Walk

Two of Old Delhi's most fascinating sights are linked by one of the largest, busiest and most compelling markets in India; the atmosphere is at its best in early evening when it is cooler and the crowds are out in force.

Although the route described keeps to the larger roads, take the opportunity to wander through the tiny side streets that make up the core of the market. The area is not large, so even if you get lost you should emerge near a recognisable landmark. *Allow about 1 hour, plus browsing time.*

Start beside the Lahore Gate of the Red Fort (see page 38). Cross the open ground and the main road opposite. During the high season, there is a fairground on this site and you may have to walk round it.

1 CHANDNI CHOWK (Silver Street)

Also known as the Moonlit Bazaar, this was the main east–west thoroughfare of Shah Jahanabad (founded 1638), a gracious boulevard with a canal and trees, that became the commercial heart of Asia. Today the street and its surrounding maze of alleys and passages are a heaving mass of humanity selling everything from plastic buckets to exquisite gold jewellery and perfumed oils.

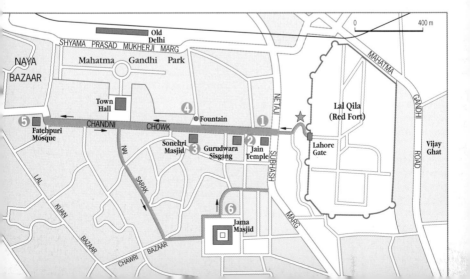

Chandni Chowk has been Main Street, Old Delhi, since 1638

On the corner of Chandni Chowk and the main road, Netaji Subhash Marg, is a Jain temple.

2 JAIN AND SIKH TEMPLES

Belonging to the Digamber sect, the balconied Parshvanatha Jain temple was built in 1650 but has been restored, extended and elaborated to such an extent that little of the original remains. It houses a bird hospital and is lit up at night. Almost next door, on the left, the white marble Sikh Gurudwara Sisgang was built in honour of the guru, Tegh Bahadur, beheaded by Emperor Aurangzeb in 1675.

The Sonehri Masjid is a little further along on the left.

3 SONEHRI MASJID (Golden Mosque)

Built in 1722, this mosque was named for its copper-clad domes. In 1739, Delhi was invaded by the Persian king, Nadir Shah, who chose to use the roof as a vantage point from which to watch as his soldiers decimated Delhi, killing many thousands (reports range from 20,000 to 150,000), looting and torching most of the city.

4 THE BRITISH INFLUENCE

On the right-hand side of the road is a small enclave of the British Raj, consisting of an ornamental fountain, colonial-style Town Hall (1860–65) and the Mahatma Gandhi Park, which leads through to Old Delhi Railway Station.

Continue down Chandni Chowk to the far end, where a narrow arch leads through the line of the old city wall.

5 FATEHPURI MOSQUE

Marking the western end of Chandni Chowk, this large red sandstone mosque was built in 1650 by Begum Fatehpuri, one of Shah Jahan's wives. Just beyond it is the spice market.

Backtrack a little way up Chandni Chowk and turn right along Nai Sarak. This road leads round the edge of the market alleys to the Jama Masjid.

6 JAMA MASJID (Friday Mosque)

See page 37.

The main entrance leads back to Netaji Subhash Marg. There are plenty of autos, rickshaws and taxis in the car park.

The Many Ages of Delhi

Most people talk of the seven cities of Delhi, based on surviving archaeological remains. However, there have definitely been up to 15 separate building periods, the area has been inhabited more or less continuously for about 3,500 years, and there is sketchy evidence of people around as far back as 15,000BC. Most surviving monuments date from the 10th century AD onwards and are found in two clusters; one in the far south and the other in the northeast of the city.

The following is not a tour but a suggested chronological itinerary; to visit them in order would not necessarily make geographical sense because of the huge distances in heavy traffic. *If you wish to do all the sights listed, allow two days.*

1 INDRAPRASTHA (15th century BC)

A legendary city of the great Hindu epic, the *Mahabharata*, the real-life prototype is thought to have been on roughly the same site as the Purana Qila (see page 53). No physical remains have been found, although the site has yielded pottery of the right age.

2 LAL KOT (late 10th century AD)

Although there are signs of habitation back as far as the 8th century, the remaining walls of this once formidable citadel are considered to mark the first surviving city of Delhi, founded by the Rajput Tomar dynasty and known at the time as **Dhilli** or **Dhillika** (the basis for the modern name). The city was captured and extended by the Chauhan family, under whom it became known as **Rajpithora**, and in 1193, by Qutb-ud-Din-Aibak, marking the end of Hindu rule in Delhi. Most of the Hindu

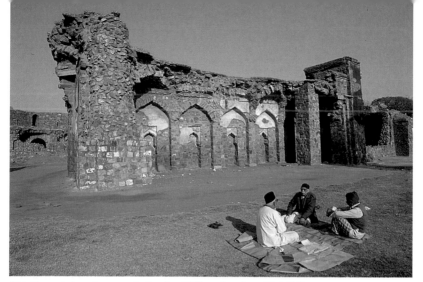
Only the central court now marks the site of 14th-century Feroz Shah Kotla

buildings were dismantled and reused in building the **Qutab Minar** complex (see page 44) which now stands on the spot.

3 HAUZ KHAS (1303)

Siri, the official second city of Delhi, was laid out by the Sultan Ala-ud-Din Khalji and was the first to be built from scratch by a Muslim ruler. All that remains are some stretches of the curtain wall and a vast tank (reservoir) known as the Hauz Khas, a little way from the city proper, which was designed to provide a safe water supply for the population. Most of the buildings in the existing complex, including a mosque and *madrasa* (religious training college), were actually built by Feroz Shah Tughluq (reigned 1351–88) whose tomb is one of several inside.

4 TUGHLUQABAD (1321–25)

An octagonal sprawl of 6.5km of 10–15m-high rubble-filled walls and 13 gates, the formidable fortress of Tughluqabad was built by Ghiyathu'd-din Tughluq (1321–25), but was only inhabited for five years. On the edge of Delhi, the massively impressive ruins are now virtually deserted, except for a few goats, and prove an excellent site for picnics and walking. On the opposite side of the road is a small walled enclosure, with a monumental gate; this was once surrounded by an artificial lake and reached by a causeway. Inside are the self-built domed **tomb of Ghiyathu'd-din Tughluq**, his wife and son, and several smaller tombs. On a nearby hill are the remains of an additional fort, **Adilabad**, built by his son, Muhammed bin Tughluq (reigned 1325–51).

5 JAHANPANAH (early 14th century)

Once he had managed to get rid of his father (with an 'accidentally' collapsing canopy during a victory celebration), Muhammed bin Tughluq went on to build yet another citadel, partway between Siri and Lal Kot. Only a few scattered walls remain of this structure.

6 FEROZ SHAH KOTLA (1354)

The Tughluqs seemed to think it necessary to build a new capital for each new reign. Feroz Shah's contribution was

The mysterious Lodi dynasty left only a few tombs to mark their reign

Hauz Khas: access via the Village Bistro (see page 156).
Tughluqabad: 8km east of the Qutab Minar, Badarpur Road.
Feroz Shah Kotla: near the Raj Ghat, Bahadur Shah Zafar Marg.
Lodi Gardens: Lodi Road.
Purana Qila: opposite the Craft Museum, Pragati Maidan.
All the sights are open daily, sunrise to sunset. Admission charge for Purana Qila, Feroz Shah Kotla and the Red Fort.

the city of **Ferozabad**, of which only the central court remains as much of the city was recycled to build Shah Jahanabad.

ASHOKAN RELICS

The Mauryan emperor Ashoka (268–231BC) was a relatively benevolent and very efficient father figure who created roads and rest houses, and sent Buddhist missionaries out to other areas of Asia. Across his kingdom, he scattered a series of pillars and rocks, carved in Brahmi script, both as a record of his achievements and exhorting his subjects to behave well. The script was finally deciphered by James Princep in 1837.

Delhi's two Ashokan pillars now stand in the grounds of Feroz Shah Kotla and beside the Hindu Rao Hospital, Rani Jhansi Marg. There is also a rock edict on an outcrop near Srinivaspuri, near the Ring Road past Lajpatnagar. Open access.

The surviving perimeter wall had four gates, one leading to the river. The buildings inside look a little like a broken down brickworks, but include a vast *baoli* (stepped well) and a sort of stepped pyramid, built to display one of two **Ashokan pillars** moved to Delhi by Feroz Shah.

7 LODI GARDENS (late 15th–early 16th century)

This delightful park, laid out by Lady Willingdon in the 1930s, contains several small tombs and mosques belonging to the Lodi Dynasty (1451–1526) who first moved their capital to Agra and then lost their country to the Moghuls. Among the tombs, those of Muhammed Shah Sayyid (1434–44) and Sikander Lodi (1489–1517) are similar, with an octagonal central chamber surrounded by arches and a high dome. The anonymous **Shish Gumbad** (Glass Dome) and **Bara Gumbad** (Big Dome) are square and have a false second storey. The mosque next door was built in 1494. The **Athpula**, a low multi-arched bridge over the stream, was probably built during Akbar's reign (1556–1605) by a nobleman, Nawab Bahadur.

8 PURANA QILA (1534)

This site has had several incarnations, beginning with Indraprastha (see page 50). Remains from the Gupta, Rajput and Delhi Sultanate periods have also been found. The Moghul Emperor Humayun built his new city of **Dinpanah** here. In 1540 he was deposed by the Afghan Sher Shah who knocked it down and built the existing fort instead, a rough rectangle with 2km of walls and three main gates. Humayun completed the fort on regaining his throne, then fell down the steps of the **Sher Mandal**, the double-storey octagonal tower which he used as a library, to a tragic death. The richly ornamented **Qal'a-i-Kuhna Masjid** (Mosque of the Old Fort) was built by Sher Shah in 1541. There is a small site museum.

9 SHAH JAHANABAD (1638–48)

This is the surviving city of Old Delhi, built by Shah Jahan (of Taj Mahal fame). See pages 38–9 and 48–9.

10 NEW DELHI (1931)

At the Delhi Durbar of 1911, King George V announced plans to move the capital of India back to Delhi. Sir Edwin Lutyens was hired to oversee the creation of yet another purpose-built capital, which was inaugurated in 1931 (see pages 46–7).

Sir Edwin Lutyens' Rashtrapati Bhawan

THE GREAT MOGHULS (1526 – 1707)

BABUR (1494 – 1530) (1526 IN INDIA)

Babur (The Tiger), the conqueror of India and the first Moghul emperor, was a great warrior, a diarist, an enthusiastic hunter, a lover of gardens and was little impressed by what he saw of his new territory. He died in the Ram Bagh gardens, Agra, and is buried in Kabul, Afghanistan.

HUMAYUN (1530 – 40, AND 1556)

Humayun is remembered chiefly for his failures. In 1540, the Afghan leader Sher Shah usurped his empire and he only retrieved it six months before he fell down his library steps to his death in 1556. His main achievement was the introduction of Persian miniature painting whose influence, combined with native Indian skill, created the classic Moghul artistic tradition. He is buried in Delhi (see page 36).

AKBAR (1556 – 1605)

The greatest of them all, Akbar came to the throne aged 13. He conquered massive new territories, including much of Rajasthan, created a proper administrative system, introduced standard weights and measures, tax structures and a workable police force. Married to at least seven wives, among them a Rajput Hindu princess from Jaipur, he was enormously liberal for his time, promoting religious tolerance, abolishing slavery and discontinuing enforced *sati*. He eventually created his own short-lived hybrid religion, *Din-i-Ilahi*, which combined elements of Islam, Hinduism, Christianity and Zoroastranism. He died in Agra and is buried in Sikandra (see page 64).

JAHANGIR (1605 – 27)

Jahangir (Conqueror of the World) contributed little to the political or territorial expansion of the empire, and is best known for his excessive use of alcohol and opium. His favourite wife, Nur Jahan (Light of the World), was a woman of staggering beauty and intellect who effectively ran the empire. He is buried in Pakistan.

Left: Shah Jahan, a great lover and great builder
Above: Humayun, like all the Moghul Emperors, has a truly palatial tomb
Right: Life at court was luxurious, surrounded by fine gardens, art, music and beautiful women

SHAH JAHAN (1628 – 58)

Shah Jahan (Ruler of the World) inherited a near bankrupt empire. Nevertheless he succeeded in expanding his territory southwards across the Deccan Peninsula and became the greatest of the Moghul builders, creator of the Taj Mahal (see page 60).

Shah Jahan spent the last eight years of his life (1658–66) imprisoned by his son within his own fort in Agra, gazing down the river at the mausoleum where he was eventually to be buried alongside his favourite wife.

AURANGZEB (1658 – 1707)

An imposing but unpleasant character, Aurangzeb (Ornament of the Throne) fought his brothers for supremacy (later executing them), then overthrew his father. A series of military campaigns extended the empire into the deep south of India, but Aurangzeb was a puritanical extremist who treated the Hindus harshly, often destroying their temples and replacing them with mosques; his policies created hatred and led eventually to a series of insurrections that fragmented the Moghul Empire. He is buried in Aurangabad, near Bombay.

Agra

*S*tanding on the Yamuna River, Agra is a city of over a million inhabitants. Like Delhi, it has been inhabited for thousands of years and takes its place in the great Hindu legends. Sikander Lodi moved his imperial capital here in 1504 and for the next 150 years, under the rule of the early Moghul emperors, the fame of its sumptuous court spread across the world. In the 1650s, however, power moved back to Delhi; in the 18th century, Agra was repeatedly attacked and pillaged by Jats and Marathas; and in 1857, it was badly damaged during the Mutiny. Today, it is a large, scruffy, chaotic and generally uninspiring city in which a handful of truly superlative buildings remain as ghosts of glory past.

Agra is 196km south of Delhi, with good road, rail and air connections.
Government of India Tourist Office, 191 The Mall (tel: 363 959); Uttar Pradesh Government Tourist Office, 64 Taj Road *(tel: 360 517/364 439); Tourist Reception Centre, Agra Cantt Station (tel: 364 439).*

The tiny but perfect tomb of Itimad-ud-Daulah proved inspirational to builders of the Taj Mahal

AGRA

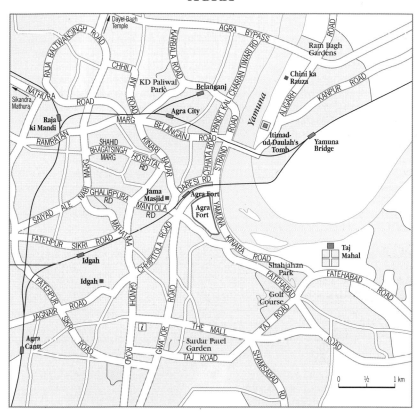

ITIMAD-UD-DAULAH'S TOMB

Composed of pure white marble inlaid with precious stones and covered with filigree screens, this tomb seems as fragile as an ivory jewellery box. Built between 1622 and 1628 by Nur Jehan (wife of Jehangir) for her Persian father, Mirza Ghias-ud-Din Beg, it stands in formal *char bagh* gardens and is as intensely, yet delicately, decorated inside as out.

Aligarh Road (east bank). Open: sunrise to sunset. Admission charge.

RAM BAGH GARDENS

Laid out by Emperor Babur in 1528, this is the earliest surviving example of a Moghul garden. In spite of 45 gardeners, a lack of water and will-power have led to its virtual demise, leaving only faint outlines of its former splendour among the overgrown bushes and broken pavilions.

Aligarh Road (east bank). Locked, but officially open sunrise to sunset; wait for a gardener. Admission free.

Red Fort

*Y*oung Prince Humayun took Sikander Lodi's fort in 1526 but it was left to Akbar to demolish and rebuild it (1565–73) with a roughly triangular 2.4km, 20m-high curtain wall, faced by decorative red sandstone. An outer ring was added by Aurangzeb. Although only a third of the size, it is very similar to the Delhi Fort, being more complete and actually feeling larger and more imposing. The royal apartments are spread out along the river wall in a maze of interconnecting pavilions and courtyards. Entry is across the 10m-deep, 9m-wide moat and through the massive Amar Singh Gate.

Akbar's Palace

Immediately on the right are two interlinked red sandstone buildings, the **Akbari Mahal** and the **Jahangiri Mahal**. These royal apartments (1570) are all that remain of Akbar's original buildings and show his preferred eclectic use of design, with Hindu, Moghul and Persian details.

Shah Jahan's Palaces

Shah Jahan demolished or redesigned the rest of the buildings, using a softer and more flowing style, with creamy marble and inlay, stucco, paint and gilt instead of the hard-edged, sombre sandstone. The difference in atmosphere is startling as you walk through the prettily decorated **Shah Jahani Mahal** and enter the enchanting **Khas Mahal** (Private Palace), its décor and gleaming copper roofs carefully restored. This was a private play area for the emperor and his women, overlooking the **Anguri Bagh** (Grape Garden), a formal jigsaw pattern Moghul garden filled with fountains and water channels. Surrounding screens ensured privacy.

Beyond this is the **Musamman Burj**, a delicate octagonal tower which is not only one of the most beautiful buildings in the Fort, but the most tragic. Built by Shah Jahan for his beloved wife, Mumtaz

Mahal, he spent much of his eight-year imprisonment here and died on the balcony, gazing down the river to the Taj Mahal. The view is superb, although now unfortunately marred by the heavy pollution haze. The marble courtyard is

SITE PLAN

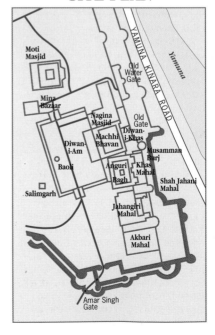

Shah Jahan filled the Red Fort with graceful, fluted marble pavilions

marked out with a Pachisi (Indian Backgammon) board, played, it is said, using dancing girls as pieces.

Beyond this, at first-floor level, are the **Diwan-i-Khas** (Hall of Private Audience), built in 1635–7, the emperors' private chapel, the **Mina Masjid** (Heavenly Mosque) and the **harem**.

At ground level, the silver-spangled **Shish Mahal** (Hall of Mirrors) is now badly damaged but was once magnificent, filled with the sound of running water while oil lamps reflected a thousand times in its glittering tiny mirrors. It led into the **Machhi Bhavan** (Fish Building), which gained its name from the central tank stocked with fish for angling. The surrounding rooms later became offices, while the courtyard was used to receive visiting dignitaries. Beside this were the emperor's baths and the **Nagina Masjid** (Gem Mosque), made of pure white marble and used by the ladies of the harem. On the far side, facing out into

the public areas of the fort, lay the **Diwan-i-Am** (Hall of Public Audience), its vast courtyard now incongruously occupied by the tomb of John Colvin, former Lieutenant-Governor of the North-West Provinces (died 1858).

The rest of the fort is closed and you can only see the domes of the supposedly perfect marble **Moti Masjid** (Pearl Mosque), built between 1646 and 1653.

Jama Masjid

Built in 1648 by Shah Jahan's favourite daughter, Jahanara Begum, this beautiful sandstone and marble mosque was intended to link the palace and the town. It stands near the Delhi Gate (now closed; no access from the fort).

The Red Fort is on the west bank, about 2.5km north of the Taj Mahal, off Yamuna Kinara Road. Open: daily, sunrise to sunset. Admission charge. Jama Masjid, on Jama Masjid Road, behind Agra Fort Station. Open access.

Taj Mahal

O Soul, thou art at rest. Return to the Lord, at peace with Him and He at peace with you. So enter as one of His servants. And enter into His garden.
89th chapter of the Qur'an,
engraved above the Great Gate of the Taj Mahal

To the 19th-century poet, H G Keene, the Taj was 'An aspiration fixed, a sigh made stone'; the British Governor General, Lord Bentinck (1828–35), planned to dismantle it and auction bits off. For all the pictures and all the words, nothing can compare with that first glow as the minarets capture the pearly pink of early dawn. Even at midday, swarming with tourists, the Taj Mahal really does remain one of the most beautiful and romantic buildings in the world.

The atmosphere alters with the changing light, so try and return several times, particularly at dawn and sunset. Also head across to the far bank to see it reflected in the Yamuna River.

Monument to love

Mumtaz Mahal (Chosen One of the Palace) was a title given to Arjumand Banu, the favourite wife of Emperor Shah Jahan (1628–58). She died in 1631, aged 39, during the birth of her 14th child. They had been married for 17 years. Her grieving husband set about creating for her the perfect mausoleum. It took 20,000 workmen nearly 22 years to complete, among them the Persian architect, Isa Khan.

The tomb is set in formal gardens, quartered by water courses and surrounded by a high sandstone wall with three gates. There is a small museum in the west gatehouse. On either side of the central platform are identical red sandstone pavilions; that on the left (west) is a mosque, the one on the right is a copy, built for the sake of symmetry.

The mausoleum itself is constructed from white marble brought from Jodhpur (300km away), and the entire building is inlaid with delicate *pietra dura* patterns and flowers, using rich red carnelian from Baghdad; red, yellow and brown jasper from Punjab; green jade and crystal from China; rich blue lapis lazuli from Afghanistan and Sri Lanka; turquoise from Tibet; gold crysolite from Egypt; amethysts from Persia; agates from Yemen; dark green malachite from Russia; diamonds from Golconda; and mother of pearl from the Indian Ocean. Shah Jahan is buried beside his wife in an underground chamber. Only false tombs under the 73m dome are on display.

The Taj Mahal is on the Taj Road. Open: daily, sunrise to 7pm. Admission and photo charge. Take a torch to see clearly inside.

POLLUTION

In recent years, the building has begun to suffer appallingly from the corrosive effects of air pollution. Not only are the authorities planning a comprehensive restoration programme, but in an unparalleled, hugely expensive and controversial scheme, are trying to relocate all Agra's industry outside the city, hopefully leaving the mausoleum out of harm's reach.

AGRA ENVIRONS

FATEHPUR SIKRI

In 1568 the much married but childless Emperor Akbar (see page 54) asked a Sufi mystic, Sheik Salim Chishti, for help. Shortly afterwards, his first son (Jahangir) was born. In gratitude, between 1570 and 1582 Akbar built this massive 7.5 sq km administrative capital around his home. For 16 years it was one of the most glamorous cities in the world, but water was short, the emperor's wars led him elsewhere and the city was abandoned. It is a compelling place, with hundreds of ruins. There are two sections: the mosque complex and the palace, a complicated series of pavilions and courtyards.

Jami Masjid

An 84-room colonnade surrounds three sides of the huge mosque courtyard. On the fourth side is the mosque itself, many of its pillars carved in Hindu fashion. Behind the mosque, a gateway through the old 6km curtain wall overlooks a spiky tower, the **Hiran Minar**, tomb of Akbar's favourite elephants (who doubled as executioners). Entry to the courtyard is through the eastern **Badshahi Darwaza** (King's Gate). In 1573, Akbar conquered Gujarat, renamed his city Fatehpur Sikri (City of Victory) and built the massive 54m-high **Buland Darwaza** (Victory Gate) in the south wall (left on entry; go outside for the full effect). Beside it is a huge *baoli* (stepped well).

FATEHPUR SIKRI

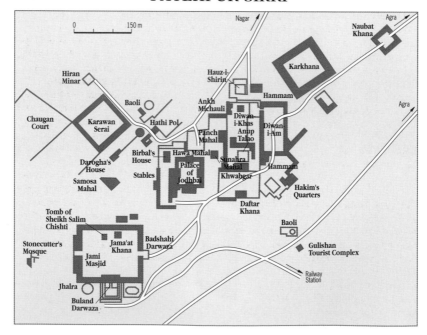

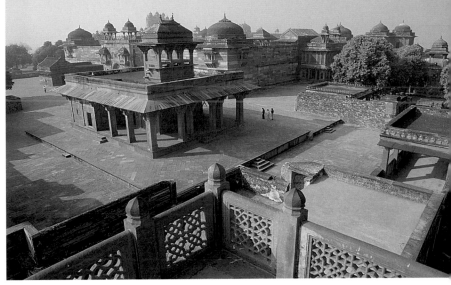
Akbar's planned city of Fatehpur Sikri was abandoned after only 16 years

Sheikh Salim Chishti's Dargah

Originally built in 1580 in red sandstone, this charming domed building is the tomb of Akbar's Sufi benefactor, who died in 1571. In 1606, Jahangir's brother clad the building in marble and added the superb latticed screens, each different and carved from a single block. Those who wish for children tie a red and yellow string to the screens and pray. Next door, the saint's sandstone **Jama'at Khana** (prayer hall) became a tomb for his family.

Palace Complex

As you enter past the ticket office, the area to the left is the **Haram Sara** (harem). Straight ahead, the freestanding **Sunahra Mahal** (Maryam's House) was the home of Akbar's mother, Maryam Makani. To the left, the rather forbidding rectangular building, with a blue tiled roof, known as **Jodhbai's Palace** (after Akbar's Hindu wife), provided the main women's accommodation. Behind it are the old **stables** and **Birbal's House**, the home of Akbar's two senior wives. Back inside, a series of small courtyards leads through the harem gardens to the open-sided five-tiered **Panch Mahal** (Wind Tower), a pavilion from which the ladies could watch the court. There's an excellent view from the top across the huge **Pachisi Court**, marked with a type of backgammon board, played, according to legend, using servant girls as pieces. To the left are the **Ankh Michauli** (Treasury) and the **Diwan-i-Khas** (Hall of Private Audience), which is dominated inside by an ornate pillar surrounded by flying arches. The emperor sat in the centre, balancing the views of his ministers who were spread along the bridges. On the far side is the **Diwan-i-Am** (Hall of Public Audience), where the emperor would hold court, and behind that were his private apartments. To the right, steps lead into the **Anup Talao** (Peerless Pool) courtyard, its central fountain pool crossed by catwalks.

37km west of Agra, on the Jaipur Road. Open: sunrise to sunset. Admission charge. Start early, wear comfortable shoes and carry water.

MATHURA

As the birthplace of Lord Krishna, Mathura is an immensely important Hindu pilgrimage centre. Several surrounding villages, including **Brindaban**, **Gokul**, **Mahaban** and **Goverdhan** are also associated with key events in the god's life and the area is littered with thousands of small temples, few of any architectural significance. The **Government Museum** has a good collection of sculpture, terracotta, bronze and coins (5th century BC to 12th century AD).

54km north of Agra, on the Yamuna River and main Delhi Road. Reached by road and rail. Government Museum, Dampier Nagar. Open: Tuesday to Sunday, 10.30am–4.30pm (7.30am–12.30pm, April to June). Admission charge.

Akbar's mausoleum, Sikandra, uses Hindu, Muslim and Christian symbols

SIKANDRA (Akbar's Mausoleum)

Emperor Akbar (see page 54) began building his own magnificent mausoleum in 1602. Composed of local red sandstone and marble, the complex has a high curtain wall with four gates, three of them dummies, and formal *char bagh* gardens, now inhabited by over-friendly monkeys.

On a raised platform at the centre, the superb five-storey stepped tomb is shaped like a Buddhist Vihar and surrounded by 44 rooms. A small strip of the once fabulously painted, central domed echo chamber has now been restored for effect. Outside, the buildings are all richly decorated with grey, black, white and yellow Rajasthani marble inlay. Recurring decorative themes include the round Hindu cupola, the minarets of Islam and the Christian cross.

Mathura Road, 15km north of Agra. Open: daily, sunrise to sunset. Admission charge.

SOAMI BAGH (Dayel Bagh Temple)

Determined to have the biggest and best in the vicinity, followers of Soamiji Maharaj, founder of the Radhasoami faith, have been building this extraordinary tomb and temple since 1904, and aren't due to complete it for another 40 years. With every conceivable form of decoration, the end result is overblown and gaudy but it is fascinating to see the traditional craftsmen in action.

Dayel Bagh Road, 3km northeast of Agra. Open: daily, 9am–5pm. Admission free.

Ajmer

A large city with a population approaching 500,000, Ajmer was founded by Raja Ajai Pal Chauhan in the 7th century. In 1193, Prithviraj, last of the Chauhan rulers, lost it to Mohammed Ghori and it became part of the Delhi Sultanate. After centuries of passing between the Muslims and Rajputs, Akbar captured the town in 1556 and made it his own Rajput base. Jahangir and Shah Jahan both lived here for some time. As a result, modern Ajmer is a real anomaly – a primarily Muslim holy city at the heart of die-hard Hindu Rajasthan. On the collapse of the great Moghuls, Ajmer passed into the control of Jodhpur, then the Marathas, and in 1818 it became a direct-rule British territory. The greatest British legacy was the Mayo College, an exclusive boys' public school opened in 1874 and still one of the finest in India.

Ajmer is 131km west of Jaipur and 205km east of Jodhpur. Tourist information office, Hotel Khadim, Savitri Girls College Road (tel: 21626).

ADHAI-DIN-KA-JHONPRA

Mohammed Ghori's commander, Qutb-ud-Din-Aibak, built this dramatic mosque in 1200, theoretically in two and a half days. In fact, he knocked down a Sanskrit College built 50 years before by the Chauhan king, Visaldeva, and reused the pieces. Each of the tall ornate columns is made up of three Hindu pillars. The superb façade, with seven massive arches inscribed from top to toe with Koranic script, was added by Iltutmish in about 1213.

About 250m north of the Dargah Sharif, Nalla Bazaar. Open access during daylight hours. Admission free.

AKBAR'S PALACE

Also known as the Daulat Khana (Abode of Wealth), this red sandstone palace was built by Akbar as his local base. It was used as an arsenal by the British from 1818 to 1862 and now houses a very second-rate Government Museum with miniature paintings, Moghul arms and 4th- to 12th-century temple statuary. *Station Road. Open: 10am–5pm, closed Friday. Admission free.*

Flower sellers line the market streets around the Dargah, Ajmer

The holy town of Pushkar has the only temple to Brahma in India

Chishtiya monastic order dedicated to protecting the poor. The complex surrounding his magnificent domed marble tomb, with silver rails and gates, was founded by the Delhi Sultan, Iltutmish, and completed by Humayun. Shah Jahan built the inner marble mosque and Akbar the mosque in the outer court. The vast cauldrons are used to feed pilgrims during the annual six-day festival, the Urs Ajmer Sharif. *Dargah Bazaar. Open, free access.*

NASIYAN (SONI) JAIN TEMPLE
Behind the temple proper, built in 1864 (closed to non-Jains), the two-storey Svarna Nagari Hall houses a fantastic gilded model depicting the Jain concept of the universe (see page 21). It took 25 years to complete and was first displayed in 1895. At the centre of the flat earth stands Mount Sumeru surrounded by the 13 continents and 13 oceans described in Jain scriptures. Above fly the airships of the Devas, coming to celebrate the five great events (Kalyanakas) – conception, birth, renunciation, attainment of omniscience, and salvation – in the life of Lord Rishabdev, first of the 24 *tirthankars*. *Anok Chowk, Seth Moolchand Soni Marg. Open: summer, daily, 8am–5.30pm; winter, daily, 8am–5pm. Admission charge. Buy the small guidebook for a detailed explanation of the model.*

TARAGARH (Star Fort)
A ruinous rectangular fort on top of a 250m-high hill, the 7th-century Taragarh is the earliest Rajput fort in existence, although most of its surviving components are considerably later. It was

ANA SAGAR
Nearly 13km in circumference, this beautiful artificial lake was built between 1135 and 1150 by Anaji Chauhan. Centuries later, the Moghul emperors Jahangir and Shah Jahan laid out a lush pleasure garden and built a series of delightful, recently restored marble pavilions along the bank. Do read the extraordinarily long list of prohibitions on the park signs. *Circular Road. Open: daily, 7am–10pm. Admission free.*

DARGAH SHARIF
The *dargah* of Muslim Sufi saint, Khwaja Muin-ud-din Chishti (1142–1236), has become a global focus of Islamic pilgrimage. Born in Persia, the saint came to India with Mohammed Ghori, settled in Ajmer and founded the

used as a sanitorium during the period of British rule.

Buildings of interest include a mosque and the *dargah* of a Muslim saint, Miran Sayyid Hussain. There are wonderful views from the top.

3km north of the city, from Nalla Bazaar. Access on foot only (allow 1½ hours for the steep climb).

AJMER ENVIRONS

PUSHKAR

For most of the year, Pushkar is a tiny peaceful town set in the hills round a deep blue lake which is said to have been formed by a falling petal when Brahma slew the demon Vijra Nabh with a lotus. Brahma went on to perform *yagna* (sacrifice) here, marrying a local girl. His wife, Saraswati, was furious and cursed him, saying that only here would he be worshipped from now on. Sitting among the 400 temples, numerous *ashrams* and *chhattris* and 52 *ghats* crowded around the lake is the only temple to Brahma in the whole of India.

As a Hindu holy place, Pushkar has a steady trickle of pilgrims and it is popular with budget travellers who come here to laze and recuperate. All that changes every October/November, however, when for two weeks the little town seethes with hundreds of thousands of people, cattle, camels and horses, gathered together for the **Pushkar Mela**, Rajasthan's biggest and most colourful fair (see page 159).

12km north of Ajmer. No tourist office, except during the fair. The town is alcohol-free and strictly vegetarian.

This massive cauldron is used to feed pilgrims to the Dargah Sharif, Ajmer

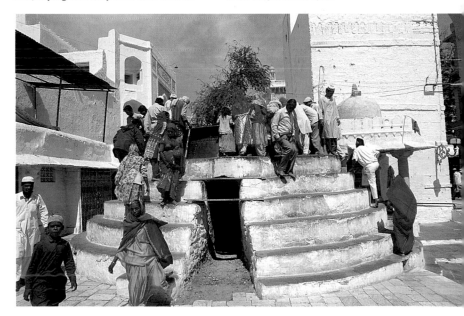

Alwar

A dusty, run-down town in the Aravalli Hills on the borders of Rajputana, Alwar has a noble pedigree, being mentioned as a powerful kingdom in the *Mahabharata* (*c* 1500BC) and by the Chinese traveller, Hiuen Tsang (7th century AD). For centuries the area belonged to Jaipur and then Bharatpur, but in 1770 Pratap Singh, a minor relative of the Kuchwaha family, broke away and set up his own kingdom which rapidly became known for its spectacular ostentation and culminated in such glories as a gold car and solid silver dining table. It is now largely ignored in favour of nearby Sariska National Park.

202km from Delhi and 141km from Jaipur, reached by road and rail. Tourist Information Office, Nehru Bal Vihar, opposite Purjan Vihar Garden (tel: 21868).

BALA QUILA FORT

Sitting 300m above the town, this superbly sited ancient fort offers fabulous views. It has massive 13km-long walls with numerous bastions and seven gates, and a richly ornamented palace complex added in the late 18th century. Unfortunately, it also houses a police transmitter and access requires special permission.

Access on foot up a steep path or by 4WD vehicle only. Ask for permission at the Collector's Office, City Palace.

VINAY VILAS (City Palace)

Built by the victorious Pratap Singh in 1771, the architecture of this vast and magnificent palace, set around two huge courtyards, shows strong Moghul influence. Most of the buildings are now used as the city's administrative offices.

On the first floor, the **Government Museum** is one of the best in Rajasthan, with a hoard ranging from a gold bicycle, old shoes and a dead tiger to an impressive and valuable collection of 18th- and 19th-century miniature paintings – including erotica of the home-grown Alwar school. Among a great many rare manuscripts are a copy of the *Mahabharata*, written on a 75m-long scroll, the *Babur Namah* (the Emperor Babur's autobiography) and works in Sanskrit, Arabic, Persian and Urdu (the court language, which was similar to Hindi but written in Persian script with some Persian words). The armoury includes some magnificent jewelled weapons, among them the swords of Akbar and Jahangir, and the armour of Mohammed Ghori.

Sagar

Surrounded by steps and elegant pavilions, this large, startlingly pea-green tank provided the City Palace's main water supply, used for drinking, bathing and laundry. To one side stands the **Cenotaph of Musi Maharani**, a magnificent memorial built by Vinay Singh in 1815 to the mistress of Bakhtawar Singh who committed *sati* here.

Open, free access to the courtyard, sagar and cenotaph. The museum is open: 10am–4.30pm; closed Fridays. Admission charge.

ALWAR ENVIRONS

BAIRAT

There is little to see, but this is one of the

The huge tank behind the Vinay Palace is still used for drinking, washing and swimming

oldest archaeological sites in Rajasthan with Stone Age cave dwellings, temples to Bhima and Hanuman (heroes of the *Mahabharata* and *Ramayana*), and a Buddhist temple and rock edict of the Emperor Ashoka (3rd century BC). *66km from Alwar on the Jaipur Road. Open, free access.*

SARISKA

This is one of Rajasthan's largest, most important and beautiful national parks. *For details, see pages 140–1.*

SILISEH LAKE

This truly delightful horseshoe lake covers an area of 10.5 sq km in a bowl of rocky hills. Beside it is a tiny water palace said to have been built by Maharaja Vinay Singh in 1810 for a young wife, a stunningly beautiful but homesick village girl who insisted on living in sight of her family. It is now a tourist bungalow, popular with monkeys. *13km southwest of Alwar, off the Sariska road. Open, free access. Boat trips and pedaloes for hire, sunrise to sunset.*

Bharatpur

*O*nce capital of the tiny kingdom of Mewat, Bharatpur's glory years began – and ended – with the 18th-century Jat ruler, Maharaja Suraj Mal, who, in 1763, helped sack the Delhi and Agra forts, coming away with several souvenirs. He also built himself a wonderful fort, summer palace (at nearby Deeg) and hunting preserve. These days Bharatpur's superlative bird sanctuary attracts many visitors, but few stray into the fort or the busy little market town, where a fascinating slice of provincial Indian life can be observed away from (most) souvenir sellers.

182km from Delhi, 54km from Agra and 174km from Jaipur, reached from all three by road and rail. Tourist information, Saras Tourist Bungalow, Agra Road (tel: 3700).

KEOLADEO GHANA BIRD SANCTUARY

In 1733 the Maharaja dammed several small rivers to create a marshlands breeding ground for birds. A stone tablet

Rickshaw-wallahs are well informed guides to the bird sanctuary

in the reserve details the staggering number of ducks the maharajahs' guests then blasted from the sky (up to 4,273 in one day during a 1938 shoot for Viceroy Linlithgow). The 29sq km area, about half of it marshland, became a national park in 1983. Now home to around 360 different species, Bharatpur is, without doubt, one of the finest bird sanctuaries in the world and has a thriving animal population. It is also beautiful, peaceful and utterly compelling even for those with no real interest in feathers.
6km from Bharatpur. Open: sunrise to sunset. Admission charge and photo charge. See also pages 72–3 and 140.

LOHAGARH (Iron Fort)

In 1732 work began on this vast and seemingly impregnable fort, with an outer mud wall 11km long. In 1805 the British failed to penetrate the defences after a four-month siege, but the Maharaja nevertheless became the first Rajasthani prince to sign a treaty. Lying within the old inner wall are three palaces, only the oldest of which is open to the public. Built on three sides of a rectangle and surrounding a sunken water garden (as usual, with no water), this now houses a rather sad **government museum** with some interesting arms, sculptures and an original *punkah* (fan). Most of the fort

walls have been destroyed.
Within the fort, access from town centre,
via Mathura Gate. Open: Saturday to
Thursday, 10am–4.30pm. Admission
charge.

BHARATPUR ENVIRONS

DEEG

The massive **citadel** was built by the Jat
ruler, Sural Mal, in 1730 and dismantled
by the British in 1804. Only the 28m-
high wall remains. In 1768 the
Maharajah built himself a stunning
summer palace of rich yellow stone
next door. The central building, the
Gopal Bhawan, is flanked on either side
by barge-shaped pavilions. In front are
lush gardens and behind it is a huge,
pea-green tank, the **Gopal Sagar**, still
used as a water supply by locals. The
palace has survived virtually intact,
furnished with its moth-eaten tigers and
billiard table, photos and various Moghul
souvenirs, such as beds, looted from the
Red Forts in Agra and Delhi.

The most fascinating aspect of all,
considering the palace's close proximity
to the desert, is the Maharajah's
obsession with water. The gardens are
filled with nearly 2,000 fountains, with
tricks and hidden jokes as well as huge
set pieces, all designed to create an
artificial monsoon. The **Keshav
Bhawan** pavilion used jets of water to
roll stone balls and recreate the sound of
thunder. For the Maharajah's birthday
celebrations, the fountains' pipes would
be packed with dye and the fountains
flowed in rainbow hues. It takes so long
to collect enough water for the
extravaganza that the fountains now only
play for three days a year, in the first
week of August.
32km from Bharatpur. There are no taxis
in Bharatpur. Provide your own transport,
or ask to borrow (hire) a private car.
Monsoon Palace open: daily, 8am–5pm.
Admission free.

Pure fantasy, the palace of Deeg created an
artificial monsoon for a thirsty desert prince

PEACOCKS AND

Left: the wild peacock is India's national bird
Below: rose-ringed parakeets wheel above the cities
Top right: treepies draw attention to themselves with their raucous call
Bottom right: Nature's bin men, vultures clean up old bones and rubbish

A gang of brilliant green parakeets screams across the city park, a scops owl tucks its head down for a day asleep and a collared dove coos softly to the dawn. The fields are dotted with ultra-white cattle egrets, scavenging for worms disturbed by the buffaloes' hooves. Bald-headed vultures huddle greedily around the village refuse dump, partridges and quails lurk plumply in the dusty undergrowth, and mina birds squabble in a nearby tree. A little black-and-white-pied robin tilts its head as it watches the watchers, busy bee-eaters follow the honey trail, a little brown bulbul trills tunefully in the bushes and a gaggle of babblers chatters about nothing. A wild peacock, India's national bird, struts past an overgrown tomb, shrieking for his hens. High above, a dozen different raptors soar on the morning thermals, eagle-eyed above the scrub.

PARAKEETS

The lakes and marshes provide a whole new range of birds, ducks and geese, moorhens and jacanas, cormorants and darters, herons, storks and cranes. A speckled pond heron floats in perfect camouflage on a muddy pool, while just above, a kingfisher flashes turquoise through the dappled shade. A mated pair of grey and scarlet Saras cranes, the world's largest birds of flight, stick close together as they feed, and, most dramatic of all, a twisted acacia tree bulges top heavy with nesting painted storks.

India as a whole is home to some 1,200 species of bird, of which at least 400 are found in and around Rajasthan. About 360 species are found in Bharatpur alone. It is a paradise for 'twitchers', the astounding range,

drama and sheer numbers of its birds sufficient to convert even Alfred Hitchcock devotees.

Bikaner

*A*fter the foundation of Jodhpur (see page 108), Jodha Rathore's second son, Bika, fought with his father and left court, heading north, deep into the desert. In 1488, he conquered Jangal Desh and founded his own kingdom of Bikaner. A hermit promised that his dynasty would rule safely for four and a half centuries, which took it neatly up to 1947 and independence.

The city survived for centuries as a staging post on the desert trade routes. Then came Maharaja Ganga Singh (1887–1943), an enthusiastic builder who achieved near saintly status. He created roads and railways, schools and hospitals and built the Gang Canal, providing irrigation for 285,000 hectares of land. At independence, Bikaner became the first Rajput kingdom to join the union. Today it is a thriving city with a population of about 450,000.

243km from Jodhpur and 321km from Jaipur, reached by road and rail. Tourist Information Office, Junagarh Fort (tel: 27445).

GANGA GOLDEN JUBILEE MUSEUM

Founded in 1937 to mark the Golden Jubilee of Maharaja Ganga Singh, the museum moved into its current home in 1954. It has a fine collection, with pre-Harappan and Gupta period archaeological finds, paintings and photographs of the royal family, and local crafts including woodwork, glass, metal pots, 'Usta' gilded leaf paintings on camel hide, fine carpets woven by prisoners in Bikaner Jail, miniature paintings and, their finest exhibit, a superb Jain marble statue of the goddess Saraswati.

Gandhi Park, Jaipur Road. Open: 10am–4.30pm, closed Friday. Admission charge.

JUNAGARH FORT

Built on flat ground in 1588 by Maharaja Rai Singh, one of Akbar's generals, the rectangular fort has a 986m-long wall, 37 bastions and a 9m-wide moat. Beside the yellow sandstone **Suraj Pol** (Sun Gate) stand lifesize statues of two warriors on elephants whose heroic feats persuaded Akbar not to attack Bikaner. This is the only fort in Rajasthan that has never

Lacy *jali* screens and ornamented stonework flourish in Junagarh Fort

View across Bikaner from the Maharaja's private apartments

been conquered. It has now been carefully restored and is filled with fabulous furniture and artistic treasures.

The low thrones in the first courtyard were used during Holi when the public were allowed to bombard the Maharaja with coloured water. The second court is much larger, decorated with elephants and Chinese and Italian tiles. On the left, inside the pretty painted gilt glass-fronted pavilion (the **Karan Mahal**), is the silver throne of the builder, Karan Singh (1631–85), a general in Aurangzeb's army. The **Anup Mahal** (Dancing Court) beyond, built by Anup Singh (1669–96) with 52 windows, one for each of his wives, was the public audience and coronation hall. Many of the surrounding rooms, and those in other palace buildings, have delightfully rich gilded floral decorations. The style, which has become the town's signature 'Usta' tradition, was introduced by Ali Raza and his family, Muslim artists from

Jaisalmer, under the patronage of Karan Singh.

The **Phool Mahal** (Flower Palace), the **Chandra Mahal** (Moon Palace) – painted to look like marble pietra dura and filled with statues of the gods – and the **Sheesh Mahal** (Mirror Palace) were built by Rai Singh in the 16th century. In the private **Fu Mahal Ki Sal** is the Maharajas' bed – too low for assassins to hide beneath and so short the maharajas would always have their feet on the ground, ready to stand and fight. Many upper rooms have superb marble *jali* screens to allow the women to watch the entertainment. Ganga Singh's 19th-century palace houses an excellent museum and armoury, including elephant howdahs, palanquins and two World War I planes. There are fine views from the roof.

Fort Road (tel: 24876). Open: daily, 10am–4.30pm. Admission and photo charge. Guided tours only.

LALGARH PALACE

Designed by Sir Swinton Jacob, and built by Maharaja Ganga Singh in 1902, this red sandstone palace is still occupied by the royal family, but most of it is now a hotel. The **Sadul Museum**'s collection of royal memorabilia includes 34,000 photographs of life at court. The **Anup Sanskrit Library** houses valuable manuscripts, many saved by Anup Singh from Golconda and Bijapur in 1687.
3km north on Lalgarh Palace Road (tel: 61963). Museum open: Thursday to Tuesday, 10am–4pm. Admission charge.

OLD TOWN

Centred on Rao Bikaji's original fort, the surviving 18th-century walls of the old town were built on the 15th-century fortifications. Within the fort are two early 16th-century Hindu temples (dedicated to Lakshmi Nath and Ganesh), the sculpted **Chintamani Jain Temple** and the magnificently painted **Bhandasar Jain Temple** – built in

The elaborately decorated interior of Bhandasar Jain Temple

1571 and dedicated to the sixth *tirthankar*, Sumatinath. From the roof there is a view of the domes, the old town and the **Bika Ji-Ki-Tekri**, cremation ground of the early rulers.
6km southwest of Junagarh Fort, along MG Road. Lakshmi Nath and Ganesh Temple, closed to non-Hindus. Bhandasar and Chintamani Jain Temples, open: daily, 7am–11.00am and 5pm–7pm. Admission free; photo charge.

BIKANER ENVIRONS

CAMEL BREEDING FARM

Bikaner is famous for its camels (see page 144). In 1975 the central government set up this station to research their habits and create a superior breeding stock. The large herds include many calves.
8km south of Bikaner. Open: 3pm–5pm, closed Sunday. Admission free.

DEVI KUND SAGAR AND CENOTAPHS

The earliest memorial in this royal cremation ground is to Kalyan Mal, who died in 1573; the latest is that of Karni Singh, who died in 1988. Other *chhatris* of note include those of the *sati*, Maharani Deep Kanwar (died 1825), worshipped as a goddess, reformer Ganga Singh (died 1943), and Anup Singh (died 1696).
8km south of city, near Camel Breeding Farm. Open, free access.

GAJNER SANCTUARY

Once a hunting preserve, the area around this lake and its 18th-century palace (built by Maharaja Gaj Singh) is now an animal and bird sanctuary, and winter breeding ground for the Siberian Imperial Sand Grouse. There are also black buck, chittal, sambar, nilgai and wild boar.
35km west of Bikaner, on Jaisalmer road. Open, free access to sanctuary. Palace open: daily, 10am–4.30pm. Admission charge.

KARNI MATA TEMPLE

This temple, with its vast silver doors and gold umbrella, is a popular place of pilgrimage but can be a trial of strength for Westerners. Within the walls live thousands of sacred rats who play over your toes. The fine for killing one is to donate a gold model of it to the temple.
Deshnok, 32km southwest of Bikaner on the Jodhpur road. Open, free access (camera charge) during daylight hours.

Karni Mata Temple, home to sacred rats

KARNI MATA

Durga, the goddess of war, came down to earth as Karni Mata for 151 years, six months and two days. Renowned as a miracle worker, she married a member of the ruling Charan family. One version of the legend says her husband's family laughed at her powers, refusing to believe in her divine nature. Goaded beyond reason, she turned them into rats. The other version is that they came to her when the young son of one of the brothers died. Karni Mata pleaded with Yama, god of death and the child was brought back to life. In exchange, however, all members of the Charan family have to live one life as a rat between human incarnations. The thousands of rather mangy rats in the Deshnock temple are, therefore, treated with great deference as honorary humans, fed by hand on sugar and grain by the many pilgrims.

Chittorgarh

*H*illtop Chittorgarh is one of the earliest and most dramatic of Rajasthan's great citadels, capital of Mewar from 728 to 1567 and a symbol of Rajput heroism. The fort was sacked three times, and each time, the men donned saffron robes and marched out to be massacred in a final hopeless battle while the women of the court flung themselves on to a giant pyre in *johar*. The fantastic figures include 50,000 killed during Ala-ud-Din Khalji's siege (1303); 32,000 men and 13,000 women and children dead during the attack by Sultan Bahadur Shah of Gujarat (1535); and a further 8,000 when Akbar triumphed in 1567. The Emperor razed the fort and it has been ruinous ever since.

Walls and Gates

The fort occupies an area of about 280 hectares (700 acres) along the crest of a 152m-high ridge, and has a 12km curtain wall. The road winds steeply up through a series of seven monumental gateways. Beside them, several *chhatris* (canopied memorials) mark the sites where famous princes and heroes fell in battle.

The Palace of Rana Kumbha (1433–68)

A typical Rajput complex of finely cut stuccoed stone, the palace has private and state apartments, horse and elephant stables, a zenana and temple to Shiva. It is said to stand on the site of Queen Padmini's *johar*. Near by are the **Nau Lakha Bhandar** (Treasury) and the 1920s **Fateh Prakash Palace,** now housing a dusty little museum.

Kumbha Shyam and Mira Bai Temples

The larger of these two temples, built by Rana Kumbha in 1448, is dedicated to Vishnu as Varaha (the Boar). The smaller was built in 1540, in honour of the Princess Mira Bai, a mystic poet and saint who dedicated her life and work to Krishna.

Vijai Stambha (1458–68)

This nine-storey, 36.6m-high Victory Tower, carved from head to toe with scenes of everyday life, was built by Rana Kumbha to celebrate his victory over the Muslim rulers of Gujurat and Malwa. Near by, the **Mahasati** is the traditional site of *sati* and the second *johar*, of Rana Karmavati.

PADMINI

Word of Queen Padmini's beauty reached Sultan Ala-ud-Din Khalji of Delhi, who became obsessed with seeing her and besieged Chittor. Eventually, to end the conflict, he was allowed to see her reflection in a silver mirror. Enflamed by the brief glimpse, he ambushed her husband and held him to ransom. Padmini capitulated and a procession of 700 veiled 'women' wound its way down to the Sultan's camp. Once inside, the Rajput soldiers threw off their disguise, routed the Muslim troops and rescued their king. The furious Sultan attacked again with greater strength. This time, the court committed *johar*, leaving Ala-ud-Din as the conqueror of ashes.

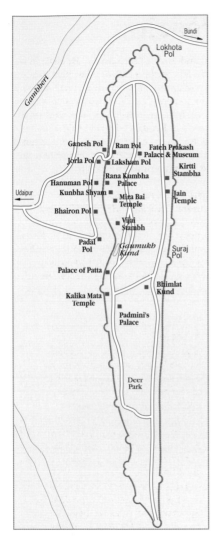

Map labels:
- Bundi
- Lokhota Pol
- Gambheri
- Ganesh Pol
- Ram Pol
- Fateh Prakash Palace & Museum
- Jorla Pol
- Laksham Pol
- Kirtti Stambha
- Rana Kumbha Palace
- Hanuman Pol
- Kunbha Shyam
- Mira Bai Temple
- Jain Temple
- Bhairon Pol
- Vijai Stambh
- Udaipur
- Padal Pol
- Gaumukh Kund
- Suraj Pol
- Palace of Patta
- Bhimlat Kund
- Kalika Mata Temple
- Padmini's Palace
- Deer Park

Vijai Stambha, 15th-century victory tower

Padmini's Palace

Complete with lotus pool and rose garden, this is actually a 19th-century reconstruction. Padmini's real story is not well documented. The popular version is the work of a 16th-century court poet. Other buildings include the 12th-century **Kirtti Stambha** (Tower of Fame), dedicated to Adinathji, first of the Jain *tirthankars*, the ruined **palaces of Jaimal and Patta**, and the 8th-century **Kalika Mata Temple**, built in honour of the sun and converted to the worship of Kalika, patron goddess of Chittor, in the 14th century.

112km east of Udaipur on the Bundi/Kota road. Tourist Information Office, Janta Avas Grih (tel: 3089). Fort open daily. Admission and video charges.

Gaumukh Kund (Cow's Mouth)

This huge hillside reservoir which gave the fort a constant water supply is now a popular swimming and diving pool for local children.

Hadoti Region

*I*n the far southeastern corner of Rajasthan, beyond the Aravalli Hills, lies the Hadoti Plateau, a fertile, well-watered land of rich black soil and highly cultivated fields. Through it flows the Chambal River, described as the Charmanyavati in the *Puranas* (ancient Hindu sacred texts), a major tributary of the Yamuna and the only Indian river which flows south to north. It now maintains four hydroelectric stations.

Geographically alien to the rest of Rajasthan, Hadoti is the traditional territory of the Hada Chauhan rulers, who moved west from Mewar conquering Bundi in 1241 and Kota in 1264. The region has a wealth of fine forts and palaces, temples and villages, but has almost dropped off the tourist map; few have heard of it, even fewer make the trek. At present, it is a green and peaceful counter-balance to the more famous cities, excellent for recouping the energy.

BUNDI

This delightful small town, named after either the *bando nal* (the twisting, steep-sided river valley in which it is situated) or *Bunda*, a 13th-century Meena chieftain, has a lake, hills and a spectacular fort, sadly in a terrible state of repair. Conquered by Rao Deva in 1241, it accepted Moghul supremacy in 1561. The town is still completely untouched by tourism, but several of the major hotel chains are talking of opening up here – as soon as the Maharaja and his sister can stop feuding about what will happen to the money generated by selling off their palaces.

39km north of Kota and 206km from Jaipur. Reached by road or, with difficulty, rail All Delhi– Bombay trains stop at Kota. Tourist Office, Circuit House (tel: 2697).

84 PILLAR CENOTAPH

This large memorial *chhatri* was built in 1633 in memory of Dhaibhai Dewa, foster brother of Rao Raja Anirudh Singh.
About 3km south of the town centre, on the Kota Road. Open, free access.

NAWAL SAGAR

In the centre of this small rectangular artificial lake, built by Rao Raja Umed Singh (1739–70), is a half-submerged temple to Varuna, Aryan god of water. The lake offers a stunning mirror reflection of the palace complex.
Below the palace. Open, free access.

Magnificent fresco in the Chittra Shala

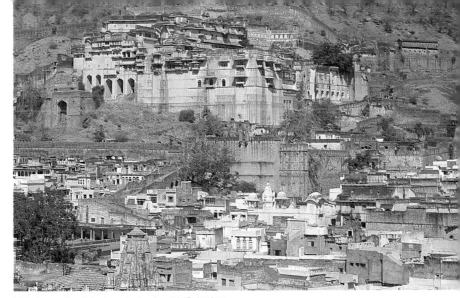

Little-known Bundi Fort equals the finest in Rajasthan

PALACE

Founded by Rao Bar Singh and finished in 1354, the hill-top **Taragarh** (Star Fort) had curtain walls, bastions and water tanks capable of withstanding a protracted siege. Below it, magnificent Rajput palaces tumble down the hillside. The precipitous path leading up to the inner court passes through the **Hazari Pol** (Gate of the Thousand), home of the palace guard, and the **Hathiya Pol** (Elephant Gate), beside which are the remnants of a water clock.

Bundi is famous for its miniature paintings, depicting flowers, trees, birds, the Ragas and Radhakrishna legends. The **Chittra Shala**, built by Rao Raja Umed Singh (1739–70), is a colonnaded quadrangle filled with joyous depictions of court life and love scenes. More frescoes can be seen by torchlight in a room behind. Other rooms include the **Badal Mahal** and **Chhattra Mahal**, built in 1632; the **Rattan Daulat**, each of its pillars topped by stone elephants,

and **Diwan-i-Am**, both built by Rao Raja Rattan Singh (1607–31). Tragically, the majority of these paintings are now deteriorating, their decay accelerated by roosting bats.

Open: daily, 10am–5pm. Admission free.
Upper section of the palace generally open.
To see the rest, you need permission from the Maharaja (ask at the Tourist Office).

RANIJI KI BAORI, see page 83.

Cycle rickshaw fit for a king

Bundi and Jait Sagar

This flat, gentle cycle ride follows a delightful lakeshore road, returning through the main bazaar. You can hire bicycles near the bus stand. The distance is about 9km. *Allow 2 to 3 hours.*

Start from the bus station. Cycle north. Take the right fork and follow the road along the town walls, past the Meera Gate, on your left, and through the terracotta Sukhi Bari Gate, to come out beside the lake. On your right is the Sukh Mahal.

1 JAIT SAGAR

Built by Rao Raja Bhij Singh in the early 17th century, this has to be one of the prettiest lakes in Rajasthan, surrounded by steep, wooded hills. Perched on the dam wall, the charming little **Sukh Mahal** (Palace of Bliss), now known more prosaically as the Irrigation Guest House, was built in 1773 as a royal guest house. Rudyard Kipling was one of its many famous visitors.

2 TOURIST BUNGALOW AND BOATS

A little further along on the left is a small tourist bungalow. There are boats or pedaloes for hire from the jetty below. On the hill opposite the bungalow is a little white mosque, the Meera Saheb, the 15th-century mausoleum of a Muslim chieftain who died here in battle.

3 TERRACED GARDEN

Next door, these pretty public gardens, opened in 1987 and festooned in bougainvillaea, were designed to provide entertainment for the locals. During the evenings they are decked out in coloured lights and blasted with Hindi film music.

Keep following the road round the lakeshore. About 2km further along, on the right, are the Kshar Bagh tombs.

4 KSHAR BAGH TOMBS

This overgrown and tangled garden is the old cremation ground of the Bundi royal family. Sixty-six *chhatris* huddle beneath the trees. The finest belongs to Chattar Sal Singh; the earliest is Kumer Duda Singh, killed in 1581.

After another 1.5km, a temple complex is reached.

5 SHIKAR BURJ

Near the road is a small, heavily restored 11th-century temple complex. The surrounding tanks are now used as the local bathhouse. Tucked into the trees behind is an old palace built by Rao Raja Umed Singh in 1770, after his abdication in favour of his son, Ajit Singh. It later became a hunting lodge and is now used as a school.

Cycle back round the lake, but take the right-hand fork along the narrow dirt road into the old city.

6 OLD TOWN BAZAAR

There are several old temples scattered among the narrow alleys and busy market stalls of the tiny town centre, but the real reason to come here is to soak up the wonderful atmosphere.

> **Kshar Bagh**: locked, but ask the gatekeeper for entry.
> **Shikar Burj**: open, free access.
> **Raniji ki Baori**: open 10am–5pm, closed Sundays. Admission free.

Bundi lake is a haven of peace and tranquillity, far from the chaos of urban India

Follow the road straight through and out of the far gate. Just beyond, beside the main road, is the Raniji ki Baori.

7 RANIJI KI BAORI

Bundi has over 50 *kunds* (tanks) and *baoris* (stepped wells). The most beautiful is the graceful, golden stone Raniji ki Baori, built in 1699 by Rani Nathawati, wife of Rao Raja Anirudha Singh. In theory nothing more than a public well, it is nearly 100m long by about 12m wide and is accessed by a steep flight of broad stairs. Above it soars a series of graceful *toran* arches decorated with friezes of marching elephants.

Turn left for the bus station and your starting point.

Kota

Sitting on the Chambal River, rapidly growing Kota is Rajasthan's biggest industrial city with a current population of about 550,000 and lush vegetation that seems to thrive on a cocktail of leaks from the local nuclear power station and belching smoke from chemical factories. The city has been ruled by the Hada Chauhans since the 13th century, a territory of Bundi traditionally held by the Maharaja's eldest son. In 1641 Shah Jahan deeded it to Rao Madho Singh as an independent kingdom, as a reward for gallant service.

245km south of Jaipur and 504km from Delhi, reached by road, rail or air. Tourist Information Office, Hotel Chambal, Nayapura (tel: 27695).

CHAMBAL GARDENS

This pleasant and beautifully maintained municipal park on the banks of the Chambal is a popular picnic spot, laid out with topiary hedges, a small zoo, crocodile pens, children's playground and a toy train.
Beside Amar Niwas, Rawat Bhata Road. Open, free access. Boats for hire.

CHHATRIS

This is one of the most attractive groups of royal cenotaphs in Rajasthan. The earliest memorial dates from 1581, the latest from the 19th century. Most are marble; all have a Shiva lingam. They are tucked under the old city walls, built of mud by Koteya Bheel, the city founder, in the 13th century, and converted into stone by Rao Madho Singh in 1580.
Kshar Bagh Gardens, beside Kishore Sagar. Open, free access.

The 18th-century Jag Mandir, Kota Lake

FORT

At the heart of the old city stands the massive fort complex, founded in 1264 by Prince Jet Singh who slew Koteya Bheel and brought the area under Chauhan rule. *Puja* is still offered daily beside Koteya's grave, near the fort gate. The massive triple wall of the fort (35 to 40m high) has six double gates. The modern entrance, through the heavy **Naya Darwaza** (New Gate), leads to **Jaleb Chowk** (Big Square), a huge central courtyard once used for military parades.

Just inside, the **Hawa Mahal** (Wind Palace) of 1864 houses a **government museum** with a variable collection of coins, manuscripts and statuary. To the left is a series of red sandstone palaces, most now home to schools and offices.

To the right, in the massive white palace complex, is the excellent **Rao Madho Singh Museum**, entered through the highly ornamental **Hathiyan Pol**. Built by Rao Madho Singh (1625–49), the decorative elephants were added to the structure by Maharao Bhim

The royal cenotaphs of Kota

Singh (1707–20). The many pavilions are delightful, decorated with marble screens, gilding, mirrorwork and crystal, while museum exhibits include paintings, furniture, costumes, photographs and armour. The miniature wall paintings are considered some of India's finest.
Government Museum, open: 10am–3.30pm, closed Friday. Rao Madho Singh Museum, open: 11am–5pm, closed Friday. Admission and photo charge.

JAG MANDIR

Lying just beyond the old city walls, the lovely Kishore Sagar lake was created in 1346 by Rajkumar Dheer Deh of Bundi. In the centre is an elegant three-storey red-and-white island palace, the Jag Mandir, built by Maharani Brij Kunwar (from Udaipur) in 1740.
Not officially open to the public, but you can hire a boat to take you over.

THE IMPORTANCE OF COLOUR

Colour has great significance in traditional Rajasthani dress. Only Rajput men can wear yellow turbans. Those of Brahmins are orange and yellow, while businessmen wear orange, lower castes dark red, and farmers and those in mourning, white. Younger women wear saris or embroidered skirts and bodices of pink, red, yellow and orange; those in black, blue, green, grey or white are widows. Saffron, the colour of purity, marks the robes worn by a *sadhu* (holy man).

HADOTI ENVIRONS

BAROLI TEMPLES (Badoli)

Built between the 8th and 12th centuries, this cluster of nine temples dedicated to Shiva stands on the banks of the Chambal River surrounded by the dense forest. The complex is thought to have been founded by Raja Hoon, of Rhysoregarh. Some of the statues have been defaced by Aurangzeb's over-zealous Muslim armies but most of the intricate carvings, particularly those in the main temple of Ghateshwara Mahadeo, are still wonderful, with a wealth of dancing girls and nymphs, and a superb image of Shiva as Natraja, Lord of the Dance.

48km southwest of Kota, near the Rawatbhata nuclear power station. Open, free access.

BIJOLIA TEMPLES

Once an important walled city ruled by the Chauhans, Bijolia was also a pilgrimage site with over 100 temples. A small village now cowers behind the walls and only three of the stunningly beautiful 10th-century temples remain standing, surrounded by fields, their ornately sculpted towers similar to those of South India. There is a giant figure of Ganesh, and a three-faced image of Shiva.

48km west of Bundi, on the Chittor/Udaipur road. Open, free access.

DARRAH GAME SANCTUARY

Covering 130sq km of the Mukundra Hills, the Darrah Game Sanctuary is home to a variety of wildlife, including

The remote 10th-century Bijolia temples are among the oldest in Rajasthan

sambar, nilgai, chittal, wild boar, hyena and leopard. Used latterly as a royal hunting preserve, the strategic mountain pass was the site of many battles. The ruined 5th-century **Bhim Chauri** temple complex includes a stone inscription commemorating a Gupta general, Dhruvaswamy, who died here in battle against the Huns. The temple is dedicated to the *Mahabharata* hero, Bhimsen, who is believed to have married the demon princess Hidimba here.
50 to 90km south of Kota, on the NH–12 to Jhalawar. Open, free access.

JHALAWAR
A small and almost totally unknown princely state, **Jhalawar** was carved off from Kota in 1838. The city itself has a fort, now used as offices, with some fine paintings and a good government museum. The **Bhawani Natya Shala** has recently been restored as a museum of Parsi theatre. In the 19th century, Raj historian, James Todd, counted 108 temples in nearby **Jhalarapatan** (City of Temple Bells). Still magnificent are the 10th-century **Surya Temple**, 11th-century **Shantinath Jain Temple**, and the group of 6th- to 14th-century **Chandramauleshwar temples**. Also near by is the formidable 8th- to 14th-century **Gagron Fort**, guarding the confluence of the Ahu and Kind rivers. Like so many other forts, this suffered various attacks, its inhabitants committed *johar*, and its useful life came to an end when conquered by Akbar in 1561.
100km southeast of Kota on the NH–12.

MENAL SHIVA TEMPLES
After his defeat by Mohammed Ghori in 1192, Prithviraj Chauhan, last Rajput ruler of Delhi, retreated to this mountain haven. Only a few stones mark his former

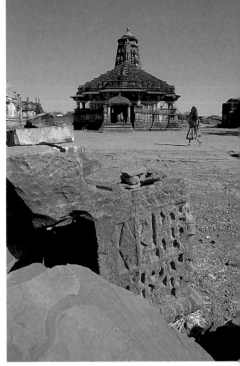

The Menal Shiva temples are all that remain of Prithviraj Chauhan's mountain fastness

palaces, but there are still several fine 12th-century Shiva temples beside the Menal River gorge. There is a really good waterfall during the monsoon, an apologetic trickle at other times.
64km west of Bundi, on the Chittor/Udaipur road. Open, free access.

RAMGARH
This complex of Shiva temples was carved from the hillside in the 10th century under the auspices of Raja Malay Verman. The main temple, 49m long by 32m wide and 32m long, was created from a single rock. The carvings of gods and goddesses outside and the erotic figures inside are slightly later and not so fine as the famous Khujuraho figures. The whole complex is deteriorating fast.
110km east of Kota. Open, free access.

Jaipur

*J*aipur (City of Jai) was built by Maharajah Jai Singh II (1699–1743), ruler of Amber (see page 94) and a true Renaissance man. Aged 11, he became the protegé of Aurangzeb and was awarded the title *Sawai* (literally 'One and a quarter'). In 1727 he and Bengali architect, Vidhya Bhattacharaya, laid out a new city following the Hindu principles of perfect architecture, as written in the *Shilpa-Shastra*, with a grid of nine blocks (two occupied by the palace). Main roads are 33m wide, with side roads down to 4m. Local aristocracy and merchants were invited in to build houses (courtyard-style *havelis*), all following an overall grand design. Different areas were set aside for different trades, in a pattern still followed today.

For a long time one of the three greatest states of Rajputana, Jaipur became capital of all Rajasthan in 1956. It is now a thriving centre with a population of about 1.5 million. Even so, the city has a laid-back, friendly atmosphere and the old 'pink city' remains intact, one of the great architectural glories of the world. Several city palaces are now hotels (see pages 172–3).

259km from Delhi, with good road, rail and air connections. RTDC Tourist Office, Hotel Swagatam Campus, near Railway Station (tel: 60586/70252); Rajasthan Government Information Bureau, Railway Station (tel: 69714). Government of India Tourist Office, Hotel Khasa Kothi , MI Road (tel: 65451).

The Rajendra Pol, City Palace

CENTRAL MUSEUM (Albert Hall)

This ornate Indo-Saracenic confection was built to commemorate the visit of the Prince of Wales in 1876 by British architect, Sir Samuel Swinton Jacob, at a massive cost of Rs 494,544. The tatty museum has some superb carpets, ivory carvings, inlay and brasswork among the plaster snakes and things in jars.

Ram Niwas Gardens (tel: 560 796). Open: 10am–4.30pm, closed Friday. Admission charge.

CHOKRI SARHAD (City Palace)

This huge complex was built at the same time as the city and has a wealth of internal furnishings and art. The ex-Maharajah still lives in part of the palace.

The **Mubarak Mahal** (Palace of Welcome), the ivory-like pavilion in the main courtyard, now houses a wonderful exhibition of musical instruments, textiles and clothes, including the awe-inspiringly large tunic and trousers of Mahajarah Madho Singh I (1750–1768), who was reputed to be 2m tall, weigh 270kg and have fathered 100 children. Along the edge of the courtyard behind the Mubarak Mahal are the photo gallery and the **Sileh Khana**, originally part of the harem and now home to the **Armoury**. The arms collection is superb and the ceilings are decorated with gold leaf, mirrors and paint. 'Welcome' in knives and 'Goodbye' in pistols are spelt out above the doors.

Flanked by marble elephants, the **Rajendra Pol** leads through to the **Sharbata-badra** (Hall of Private Audience). The two urns here are the largest silver items in the world, weighing 345kg and with a capacity of 9,000 litres. They were commissioned by Madho Singh II, who filled them with Ganges water to take on a visit to London in

The superb Peacock Door, City Palace, represents the coming of spring

1902 (he would have lost caste by drinking the polluted local version).

To the left, the **Ridhi Sidhi Pol** leads through into the **Pritam Niwa Chowk** (Dancing Courtyard), with four enchanting **Peacock Doorways**, each representing a season. The rooms beyond contain fine Moghul glass.

Back across the main courtyard, the enclosed **Diwan-i-Am** (Hall of Public Audience) is now home to the **Art Gallery**, with a fabulous array of Afghan and Pakistani carpets, Moghul and Rajasthani miniature paintings, and around 20,000 manuscripts.

Old City, off Tripolia Bazaar and Siredeori Bazaar (tel: 48146). Open: daily, 9.30am–4.45pm. Admission and photo charge. Keep ticket for use in every section.

LAKSHMI NARAYAN TEMPLE (Birla Temple)

Built by the industrialist Birla family, this gleaming white marble temple is dedicated to the goddess of wealth. The **Moti Doongri** fort, above, is the residence of the current Maharajah's step-brother.
Jawaharlal Nehru Marg. Open access.

The Hawa Mahal, five storeys high, one room deep and open to the wind

GOVINDJI TEMPLE, see page 97.

HAWA MAHAL (Palace of the Winds)

Five storeys tall, but only one room wide, this delightfully distinctive building was constructed in 1799 so that the ladies of the *zenana* (harem) could watch the outside world. Its name derives from the constant cool breeze that blew through the latticed screens on its 953 windows. On the ground floor are a small art gallery and a museum of Jaipuri history. For good photographs, visit early in the morning. The shops opposite hire their balconies and roofs to those who want a better angle.
Siredeori Bazaar (entrance to the rear) (tel: 48862). Open: 9am–4.30pm, closed Friday. Admission charge.

JANTAR MANTAR, see page 97.

MUSEUM OF INDOLOGY

An eccentric mix of ancient manuscripts, textiles, tantric art etc. Look for oddities such as Hindi script painted on a hair and a map of India on a grain of rice. *Prachya Vidya Path, 24 Gangwal Park (tel: 48948). Open: daily, 9am–6pm. Admission charge.*

NAHARGARH FORT (Tiger Fort)

Perched dramatically on a cliff, this fort, built in 1734 and extended in the 19th century, was designed to protect Jaipur and house the city treasure. The view from the curtain wall is magnificent. *Above the city; access off the Amber Road or up a steep footpath (tel: 383 202). Open: daily, 10am–4.30pm. Admission charge. Restaurant and café open all evening.*

RAMBAGH PALACE, see page 168.

RAM NIWAS GARDENS, see page 96.

JAIPUR CITY

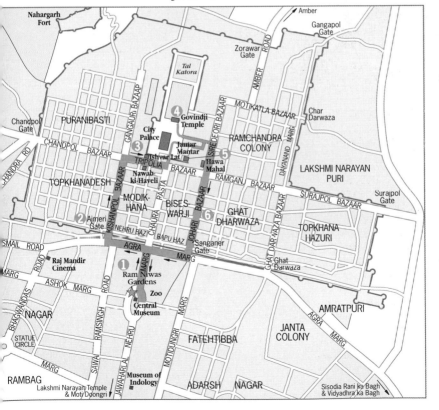

THE RAJPUTS

Mystery surrounds the origins of the Rajputs, who seem to have sprung, fully armed, from the desert sands in about the 8th century AD. They claim direct Aryan descent back to the sun, moon and fire. More probably, they were warlike pre-Aryan natives, Hun and Scythian invaders (6th–7th centuries) who received *kshatriya* (warrior/ruler) caste status in a ritual purification by fire at Mount Abu. Whatever the case, for the last 1,000 years, they have ruled Rajasthan with an iron grip.

There are 36 clans, many with familiar names – Bhatti (Jaisalmer), Chauhan (Ajmer), Hada Chauhan (Bundi/Kota), Jat (Bharatpur), Kuchwaha (Amber/Jaipur), Rathore (Bikaner/Jodhpur), and Sisodia (Udaipur). All the men, whether ruler of a single village or a great state, take the title Singh (Lord).

The Rajputs gradually carved themselves kingdoms in a welter of blood, building up a splendid legendary tradition of romance, chivalry and extravagant valour, still very much alive today. In reality many rulers were more pragmatic. Only one, Maharana Pratap Singh of Udaipur, refused to submit to the Moghuls, while the others struck deals and even intermarried. Hindu and Muslim cultures borrowed freely from each other and most of the great forts have Moghul features. The Rajputs even adopted the Islamic tradition of *purdah*, adding it to *sati* to make the lives of their women unbearable in life and

Left: Rajputs are keen hunters as well as warriors; bottom left: ex-Maharajah Surendra Singh at home in Shahpura; below: Sati prints in Bikaner mark the princesses who burnt on their husbands' funeral pyres; bottom right: royal cenotaphs in Jaisalmer

death. Their greatest heroine, Queen Padmini, led her court in *johar* (mass suicide by fire) rather than let her face be seen by a lascivious invader (see page 78).

These days the rulers have been dethroned, but many still live in palaces; some have entered politics and others are captains of industry (over 70 per cent of the tourist trade is in Rajput hands). Deeply conservative, they dream of past glories, wield immense authority – particularly in rural communities – and they are determined to hang on to their traditional, if not their legal status.

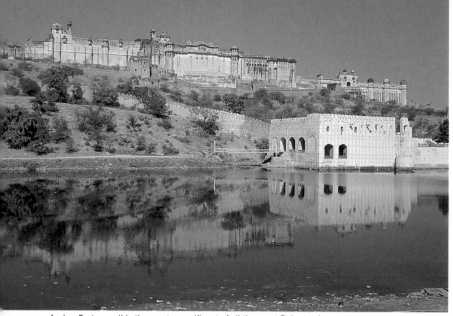

Amber Fort, possibly the most magnificent of all the great Rajput palaces

JAIPUR ENVIRONS

AMBER FORT (Amer)

The name is romantic, but the reality of this vast, magnificent fortified palace is far more so. Built in 1592 by Maharajah Man Singh, it was by no means the first fort on the site. The Kuchwaha family had reigned here since the 11th century and the surrounding hills are littered with ruins. Perilously near Agra, the family became the first of the Rajputs to agree terms with the Moghuls. Bihar Mal (1548–74) married his daughter, Jodhbai, to Akbar and sent his adopted grandson, Man Singh, to court. In return, the family reaped honours, influence and rewards. Amber's design is strongly influenced by Moghul architecture.

Views of Amber

On rounding the corner of the steep valley road, a magnificent view of the fort is seen, carved into the hillside and reflected in the waters of **Moata Sagar** (Lake Moata), with the brooding bulk of **Jaigarh Fort** (see page 99) hovering above and the formidable defensive walls marching off across the heights. Behind the lake, a steep twisting path winds up past the formal terraced **Dil-i-Aaram Gardens** to the monumental **Jai Pol** (Victory Gate).

Outer courtyards

The first court, the **Jaleb Chowk**, is filled with souvenir shops and decorated elephants. Tucked almost out of sight, beside the stairs, is the **Shila Devi Temple** – the family shrine dedicated to Kali, goddess of war, with a 16th-century Bengali image installed here in fulfilment of a vow.

The **Singh Pol** (Lion Gate) leads into the first royal court and the **Diwan-i-Am** (Hall of Public Audience), with a red sandstone canopy surrounded by carved elephants and delicately decorated walls, said to be so beautiful that they were covered in stucco to appease the envious Moghul emperor Jahangir. The terrace is a favourite hangout for monkeys. Beyond this is the vivid **Ganesh Pol** (Elephant Gate), built by Jai Singh I in 1640 and a riot of mosaic, fresco, sculpture and colour.

Private apartments

The third courtyard is filled with flowers. To the right is the **Sukh Niwas** (Hall of Pleasure), cooled by running water and fountains. To the left, the marble **Jai Mandir** (Temple of Victory) acted as the Diwan-i-Khas (Hall of Private Audience). Behind it lies Amber's greatest treasure, the **Sheesh Mahal** (Hall of Mirrors), a series of truly fabulous, glittering rooms patterned all over with mirrors and niches for oil lamps. These formed part of the emperor's private apartments. Upstairs, the little **Jas Mahal** has a superb lacey marble screen and wonderful views down the valley. Beyond this, the oldest part of the palace is in poor repair.

11km north from Jaipur, on the Delhi Road (tel: 530 293). Open: daily, 9am–4.30pm. Admission and photo charge. It is a steep climb up from the car park. Walk or hire a jeep or an elephant.

GAITOR (Jaigarh Fort), see pages 98–9.

SISODIA RANI KA BAGH

Built by Maharajah Jai Singh II in 1710 for his wife, Sisodia Rani of Udaipur, who wished to live away from court, this delicately decorated little palace, one of the prettiest in Rajasthan, is sadly closed and can be seen only from the outside.

The Hall of Mirrors gleams like stars

Its formal gardens are barely maintained. *8km from Jaipur on the Agra Road. Open: gardens, 8am–6pm. Admission charge.*

VIDYADHRA KA BAGH

Named after Jai Singh's architect and chief minister, the man who planned Jaipur, this is another sad remnant of what must have been a delightful garden in the formal Moghul style.
Opposite the Sisodia Palace, 8km from Jaipur on the Agra Road. Open: daily, 8am–6pm. Admission charge.

Take an elephant up the hill to Amber

Pink City Walk

This gentle walk takes in the best of the walled city, including the City Palace and the shopping bazaars. For the route, see the Jaipur city map on pages 90–1. *Allow about 1 hour walking, plus sightseeing and shopping time.*

Start in the Ram Niwas Gardens.

1 RAM NIWAS GARDENS

These popular gardens were laid out by the last Maharajah, Man Singh II (1922–1949), as a famine relief project. At the centre is the splendid **Central Museum** (see page 89), and near by are a small zoo and a bird park – good on atmosphere but short on animals.

Walk up towards the old town, turn left along Agra Marg, and right through the Ajmeri Gate.

2 CITY WALLS AND GATES

The imposing city wall with its seven monumental gates is for effect as much as defence. The city is built of naturally greyish-pink sandstone but its current, rather startling colour dates back to 1876 when the extravagant Maharajah Ram Singh painted the entire town to welcome the Prince of Wales (pink is the Rajasthani colour of hospitality).

Walk up Kishanpol Bazaar and turn right into Tripolia Bazaar. On your right, the Nawab-ki-Haveli is one of the finest merchants' houses in the city. A little further along, on your left, is a white tower.

3 ISHVAR LAT

This tower, the 'minaret which pierces the heavens', was built by Raja Sawai Ishwari Singh in 1749 in order to commemorate his victory over his brother, Madho Singh.

Further on, to your left, are two gateways into the palace complex. Use the smaller Atish Gate, but first have a quick look at the magnificent main Tripolia Gate, opened only for ceremonial processions. For the City Palace, see page 89.

4 GOVINDJI TEMPLE

Just north (left) of the palace, this temple was built to house an image of Govind (Krishna as a cowherd – the Jaipur family god) rescued from Mathura and the advancing Moghuls. It was designed so that the Maharajah could view the image from his terraces. There are seven ceremonies honouring the idol each day, between 5am and 9pm.

5 JANTAR MANTAR

South (right) of the main entrance is the Jantar Mantar (literally 'Instrument to Make Calculations'). Built between 1728 and 1734, this is the largest, most ambitious and best preserved of five astronomical observatories constructed by Jai Singh II, who was fascinated by science and became a world-class astronomer. It has 18 different instruments, used to plot the movement of the sun, stars and moon, and calculate time, date, season, the monsoon and the signs of the zodiac.

Leave the complex by the main gate on to Siredeori Bazaar. Turn right, and almost immediately on your right is the Hawa Mahal (see page 90). Cross straight over at the crossroads and walk down through Johari Bazaar.

6 JOHARI BAZAAR (GOLDSMITHS' MARKET)

A broad street which is seemingly crammed 24-hours a day with people and shops and traffic and camel carts, this is the most interesting of Jaipur's bazaars. Shops on both the main street and the myriad side alleys specialise in textiles and jewellery.

At the far end, Sanganeri Gate leads back through the city walls. Get a rickshaw from here, or turn right for the museum.

Zoo and bird garden. Open: March to October, daily, 8am–6pm; October to March, 8am–5.30pm, closed Tuesday. Admission charge.
Ishvar Lat is closed to the public.
Jantar Mantar. Open: daily, 9am–4.30pm. Admission charge.

Jaipur to Amber

This is the classic tour done by all visitors, linking the two great palaces of Jaipur and Amber. *Allow a very long morning to do it justice.*

Leave the walled city of Jaipur by Zorawar Gate. Shortly afterwards, a pot-holed road off to the left leads to the Gaitor (about 1km).

1 GAITOR

Tucked beneath Nahargarh Fort is the cremation ground of all the Jaipuri rulers (except Sawai Ishwari Singh), dedicated to the ruling Sun God of the Kuchwaha family. Many of the individual cenotaphs are beautifully designed, with delicately sculpted friezes and columns. The finest is the 20-pillared mausoleum of Jai Singh II (1743), carved with Hindu mythological scenes. Others of note include Madho Singh I (1768), Pratap Singh (1803) and Sawai Ram Singh II (1880).

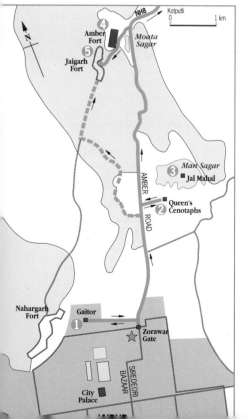

Return to the main road and turn left, continuing towards Amber. There are numerous factory shops along this road, making and selling carpets, Jaipur pottery, blockprint and other fabrics (see pages 148–55). After about 2km, on your right are the Queens' Cenotaphs.

2 MAHARANI-KI-CHHATRI
(Queens' Cenotaphs)

This is the cremation ground of the royal wives and children. While none of the mausoleums are as magnificent as those of the kings, take the time to look at the wonderful quality of the detailed carving.

A short way beyond is a small lake, nearly drowned by a sea of water hyacinth.

3 JAL MAHAL

This now inaccessible palace in the centre of the Man Sagar seems

The now flooded Jal Mahal was once a hunting lodge

impossibly romantic, but was actually an overgrown shooting hide built by Sawai Madho Singh for hunting parties.

The road now winds steeply through a mountain pass to the Amber Fort. From the car park, walk or, more easily, but expensively, take an elephant.

4 AMBER FORT
See page 94.

Dizzyingly perched above Amber is Jaigarh Fort. An almost vertical 1.5km path links the forts. To reach it by road, backtrack towards Jaipur; after you pass the Jal Mahal, a road to the right leads up the mountain. At the top the road forks; turn right for Jaigarh or left for Nahargarh Fort (see page 91).

5 JAIGARH FORT
This magnificent mountain stronghold dates back to the 11th century, but was rebuilt by Jai Singh II in 1726 as a home for the royal treasure. The taxmen hunted for six months in 1976 before concluding

---

Jaigarh Fort. Open: daily, 9.30am–4.30pm. Admission and vehicle charges. The **Cenotaphs** are open from sunrise to sunset. Admission free.

---

that it was gone. Jaipur. The fort was used as a gun foundry from 1584 onwards. The decorative Jaivana cannon, built in 1720 and claimed to be the largest in the world, has only ever been fired once, as a test, the ball travelling 38km. The museum has a fine collection of arms, many made here, displayed with histories of where they were used. The palace complex behind includes a couple of small temples and a purpose-built puppet theatre. There are truly spectacular views from around the walls.

Return to the main road to reach Jaipur.

The Gaitor, memorial to the Maharajahs

Jaisalmer

A magnificent citadel rising from Tricuta Hill like a red gold crown above the desert plain, Jaisalmer is one of the oldest Rajasthani forts. It was built in 1156 when Prince Jaisal, officially regent to his nephew, siezed power for himself and moved the capital from nearby Luderwa to this huge defensive fortress. The hermit who showed him the spot prophesied that the fort would be sacked two and a half times.

The early ruling Bhatti family behaved like bandits, looting and rustling at will. The first two attacks, by Ala-ud-Din Khalji (1308–1315) and Muhammed bin Tughluq (1325) both came in retaliation for Bhatti raids. The inhabitants committed *johar* in both cases. A final attack in the 16th century by Pathans (the half) was beaten off, but only after the Rawal had slain the women by sword. For the next two centuries, the town enjoyed relative peace and prosperity as a trade centre on camel caravan routes to the Middle East, attracting hard-working Paliwal Brahmins and Jains. New arrivals were given one rupee, one stone and one day's labour to help them get started and the town grew rich. In the late 18th century, however, it was all to change.

First the trade collapsed as the sea trade grew, then the notoriously cruel prime minister, Salim Singh (1784–1824), imposed taxes instead of voluntary donations and, even more heinously, tried to marry a Brahmin girl. The Brahmins scattered taking their wealth and cursing the town, prophesying that the monsoon would vanish forever. By the end of the century, the population had dropped from 118,000 to 4,000 and there was still terrible drought.

In 1965 India and Pakistan went to war, and strategically important Jaisalmer gained a road and air force base. In 1975 Indira Gandhi visited the base and ear-marked the crumbling town for tourist development. Today it has a railway and a rapidly growing population, is negotiating for an airport and is a highlight of any tour of Rajasthan.

295km west of Jodhpur, reached by road and rail. Central Jaisalmer is easily accessible on foot (there are no cars within the citadel). The station is nearly 5km from the town. Tourist Office, RTDC Moomal Tourist Bungalow, Collectors' Office Road (tel: 2392); 1.5km from Fort Gate, 3km from railway station. Open: 8am–noon and 3–6pm, closed Sunday.

BADA BAGH

The royal cremation grounds are set between the desert and a rain-fed lake, built by Maharawal Jai Singh II. A wheat crop is planted as the lake dries up each year. Each of the memorial *chhatris* has a central column with a bas relief of its owner. Many are followed by figures – one for each wife or consort who committed *sati* on his funeral pyre. You can see a definite progression of style from the angular shapes of the early Hindu monuments at the back (over 300 years old) to the round arches of later, Moghul-influenced architecture. This is a particularly good point from which to view the sunset.

About 2km north of Jaisalmer, off the Ramgarh road. Open access. Admission free.

Jaisalmer Fort soars above the desert, crowning Tricuta Hill

JAISALMER

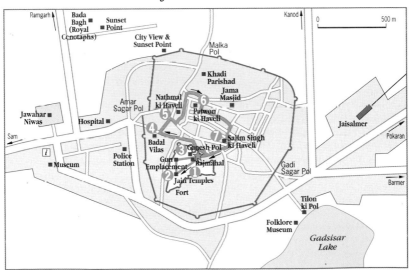

Seven gateways guard the Citadel entrance

CITADEL

Built entirely without mortar, this 12th-
to 16th-century sandstone fort tops a
triangular 76m hill with walls 6.4km long
and 9m high, while steep cliffs tumble
beneath the 99 bastions to the plain. Of
four entrances, only one is used. Four
thousand people still live within the
citadel in a maze of tiny alleys, each more
exquisitely decorated than the last.

Gates

The entrance is through several
monumental gateways. **Ganesh Pol**,
dedicated to the Elephant God, is
followed by the **Suraj Pol** (Sun Gate).
Just beyond, the **Signal Balcony** on the
right, traditionally used to play drums as a
warning of approaching visitors, was last
used as an air-raid warning during the
Indo-Pakistan Wars (1965 and 1971).
Beyond this are the **Bhoota Pol**
(Haunted Gate), with a temple dedicated
to the warlike Bhatti ruling goddess,
Bhavani, and the cool and breezy **Hawa
Pol** (Wind Gate).

City Palace

The **Dashara Chowk** is the main
market, and the place of ceremonial
sacrifice, *johar* and *sati*. Beside it, several
small 14th- to 19th-century palaces make
up the empty and crumbling **Rajmahal**.
Broken furniture litters the courtyards,
but some of the rooms still retain their
beautiful decorations, with tiles of roses,
miniature paintings and lacy marble
screens. Look in particular for the
paintings of 18th-century Jaisalmer.

Jain Temples

At the heart of the citadel stands a group
of seven interconnecting Jain temples,
built between 1470 and 1536 by wealthy
traders. Their generosity has created
magnificent works of art, with frilly
chandeliers carved from a single stone,
elaborate *toran* arches of welcome and
pillars and domes covered with a
chattering mass of sculpted girls,
dancing, singing, washing and preening.
Round the walls are friezes of elephants,
chariots and Hindu deities, depicted in
thanks to the religious tolerance of the
Maharawals. The cross-legged statues of
the *tirthankars* seem austere in their
comparative simplicity. Below the third
temple is an important library containing
466 books written on palm leaves, dating
back to the 11th century, many other
manuscripts, a statue of Mahavira (the
founder of Jainism) made of emeralds,
and a copy of the Luderwa Tree of
Imagination (see page 105).

*Open access to the citadel at all times. Raj
Mahal, Dashara Chowk. Open: winter,
daily, 8am–1pm and 3–5pm (to 5.30pm
summer). Admission charge. Jain temples,
open: daily, 8am–12 noon (library,
10am–11am only). Admission free, but
photo charge.*

Rainwater-fed Gadsisar Lake was once Jaisalmer's only water supply

GADSISAR LAKE (Gadi Sagar)

This rainwater-fed reservoir was built in 1156 and rebuilt in 1367 by Maharawal Garsi Singh. Until 1965, it remained the city's only water supply (now supplied by pipe from the Indira Gandhi Canal). The **Tilon ki Pol**, the palatial archway at the water's edge, was built by a famous local prostitute. The horrified king tried to tear it down, but staying one jump ahead, Tilon added a tiny temple to Satyanarayan (Krishna, as God of Truth) and ensured the building's survival. Along the lake shore and on the islands are a host of little temples and *chhatris*.

Folklore Museum

This delightful and informative craft museum was founded in 1984 by a local author, N. K. Sharma, and is helped on by the unbounded enthusiasm of the owner. Eclectic displays include textiles, local geology, royal ceremony, musical instruments, coins, stamps and letters, puppets and *kavads* (box theatres) *Open, free access to the lake (best in early morning). Boats for hire. The Folklore Museum is open: daily, 9am–12 noon and 3–6pm. Admission charge.*

For other sights in Jaisalmer, see **Jaisalmer Town Walk**, pages 106–7.

The narrow alleys of 'modern' Jaisalmer

Cows' dung drying for fuel

baoli (stepped pond), considered to have sacred properties, is a popular place of pilgrimage. Within the grounds are several memory pillars, records of building work, donations and so on, and a number of shrines to the Monkey God, Hanuman, giver of power.

15km north of Jaisalmer, off the Ramgarh road. Open access. Admission free.

DESERT NATIONAL PARK

Akal Wood Fossil Park

This area was once heavily wooded with non-flowering trees such as chir and deodar. About 180 million years ago (the Mezoic/Jurassic era), the sea rushed in and drowned it. When the sea retreated again about 36 million years ago, it left behind a fossilised forest. Covering about 10 sq km of bare hillside, the fossil park contains 25 petrified trunks – the largest measuring 13m long.

JAISALMER ENVIRONS

AMAR SAGAR

This is a complex site, with a Shiva temple and rainwater reservoir built in 1740 in honour of Maharawal Amar Sing (1698–1710). There are also several small temples and memorial *chhatris*. The complex of three Jain temples, built originally in the late 17th century, was badly damaged by monsoon floods and is being reconstructed. Names of financial donors are listed on the walls, and you can see stone masons in action.

7km northwest of Jaisalmer, on the Luderwa road. Open access. Admission free, but photo charge.

BAISAKHI TEMPLE

Built in the 10th century and rebuilt in the 16th, this Shiva temple, with a deep

Sam Dunes

This small 3km long stretch of billowing dunes is the only one easily accessible from Jaisalmer and, as such, is usually overrun by tourists on camel rides (see page 145). It is possible to ride away from the pack, or stay out to eat or sleep under the moon and feel the real magic of the desert sands.

30km from Jaisalmer (285km from Jodhpur). Open access to Akal Wood Fossil Park (20km from Jaisalmer on the NH15 to Barmer) and Sam Dunes (42km west of Jaisalmer). See also page 140.

LUDERWA (LODUVA)

Although this is the site of the first capital of the region, abandoned in the

Camels are the lifeblood of the desert villagers

12th century (see page 100), there are few early ruins near by and the main sight here is a wonderful Jain temple, built by Tharusha Bhansali in about AD1615 and shaped like a series of Chinese lanterns fanning out from the central portico. The *toran* (entrance arch) is from an earlier temple, destroyed by Mohammed Gori of Gujurat in the 12th century. The statue, made of touchstone (used to test the purity of gold) was made in Gujurat in the 17th century. On a column in the courtyard is a fantastic tree of wood and iron, the **Kalp Vrkasha** (Tree of Imagination). Made about 150 years ago, it is said to grant wishes to those who pray here. Stay alert as there are rats and a cobra living in the courtyard.
16km northwest of Jaisalmer. Open: daily, 8am–8pm. Admission free, but photo charge.

VILLAGES
During the rule of the 18th-century prime minister, Salim Singh, the Paliwan Brahmins abandoned 84 villages surrounding Jaisalmer. Some of them have been resettled, although by other castes or army camp followers. Others are derelict, fascinating ghost towns **Kuldhera** has been preserved as a monument to the old Brahmin communities. Nearby **Damodra** has been reoccupied and the local children are keen to show you around. **Kanoi** is now home to communities of wood-carvers and musicians.
Damodra is 15km from Jaisalmer, 20km from Kuldhera and 37km from Kanoi, all on the road to the Sam Dunes. Most tour operators run village tours. Open, free access, but baksheesh required.

Jaisalmer Town Walk

This walk provides the best possible way to see Jaisalmer, meandering through narrow lanes past the intricately carved and painted doorways of the great citadel, the crowded markets and grandiose havelis of 19th-century merchants in the new town. For the route, see the Jaisalmer town map on page 101. *Allow about 1 hour, plus browsing and sightseeing time.*

Start in the main market place beside the Ganesh Pol, and walk up through the Citadel.

1 CITADEL

For the citadel and Rajmahal, see page 102.

From the Dashara Chowk, take the lane to the right, signed Hotel Paradise, and follow it past the hotel to the Jain temples (if in doubt, follow the postcard stalls).

2 JAIN TEMPLES

See page 102.

Turn back along the lane and then go left, past the small Hindu temple of Lakshmi Nath. Beyond this, scramble up the broken-down stone stairway on to the bastion.

3 GUN EMPLACEMENTS

On the bastions several of the city's old cannons still menace the surrounding countryside. The real reason for coming up here, however, is for the superb view, which seems to stretch into forever, while eagles and kites wheel on thermals beneath the walls.

Patchwork hangings of old embroidery are one of Jaisalmer's lucrative and beautiful products

Return to the Dashara Chowk and leave the fort. Turn left at the last gate, along the line of the walls, and walk through to the Amar Sagar Gate, one of the few remaining vestiges of the old town walls. On your right is the Badal Vilas.

4 BADAL VILAS (Mandir Palace)

Current home of the royal family, the palace was built during the reign of Maharawal Jawahar Singh (1914–46). The five-storey tower was built as a present to the royal family by Muslim Silavata craftsmen before they emigrated to Pakistan during Partition in 1947. It is shaped like a Tazia (paper and bamboo models of Shia Muslim mausoleums, made to honour the deaths of the Prophet's grandsons). There are numerous temples and some massive cooking pots in the grounds.

5 NATHMAL KI HAVELI

In 1886 the Maharawal Beri Sal Singh gave this magnificent *haveli* to his prime minister, Deewan Nathmal. It was carved by two Islamic Silavatas brothers, Hati and Laloo, who designed one wing each. Each of the seven balconies on the façade is carved from a single stone. The splendid stone elephants signify the residence of a prime minister.

Continue past the haveli, *turn right and then right again along Noidani Mohelle and you will come out beside the Patwon ki Haveli.*

6 PATWON KI HAVELI

Probably the most magnificent of all, this is actually a group of five *havelis* built in the mid-19th century by the enormously wealthy Jain businessman, Guman Chand Patwa, for his five sons. The intensely ornamented façade is quite superb but immensely difficult to photograph. Inside,

The superb façade of Patwon ki Haveli is typical of Jaisalmer's ornate mansions

decorative rooms surround a balconied courtyard of glowing golden stone.

Walk through the bazaar along Acharya Mohelle and turn right to reach the third great haveli.

7 SALIM SINGH KI HAVELI

This extraordinary building has five relatively simple storeys and a fabulously decorated sixth overhanging the tower, surrounded by peacock brackets. It is the earliest of Jaisalmer's great *havelis* and home of the notorious prime minister, Salim Singh (1784–1824), who was not only a mass murderer, but almost destroyed the city (see also page 100) before he was himself murdered.

From here, it is a short walk straight up the road to the Fort Gate.

Mandir Palace, beside Amar Sagar Gate (tel: 2733/2538). Open access to courtyard only. A few rooms are run as a hotel. The *havelis* are open: 10.30am–5pm. All of them have shops inside.

Jodhpur

*B*efore independence, Jodhpur was one of the greatest of the Rajput king-doms, covering a massive 93,240sq km. The royal family claim descent from the great Deccan Rashtrakuta dynasty (8th to 10th centuries) and through them, the sun. On the fall of the Rashtrakuta kingdom, they migrated north to Uttar Pradesh, then west. Finally, in 1192, Rao Siha moved into the Thar Desert, and in 1381 Rao Chunda conquered Mandore. The desert kingdom of Marwar (Land of Death) and the modern Rathore dynasty was born.

Chunda's son, Ranmal, turned his attentions to green and pleasant Mewar, but failed and was drugged and killed during a state banquet. His son, Rao Jodha (1453–89), fled back to Marwar and shifted the capital from Mandore to the safer clifftop Jodhpur. In the late 16th century the Rathores made peace with Akbar, and were awarded the title of Raja. Like other willing subjects, they generally flourished under Moghul protection, though it caused repercussions when Jaswant Singh picked the wrong side during Aurangzeb's battle with his father, Shah Jahan, and his brother, Dara.

Jodhpur was a staging post for camel caravans linking China and the Middle East. The city grew rich on trade in silks and opium, copper and coffee, sandalwood and spice, until the arrival of

View over Jodhpur's Brahmin district

JODHPUR

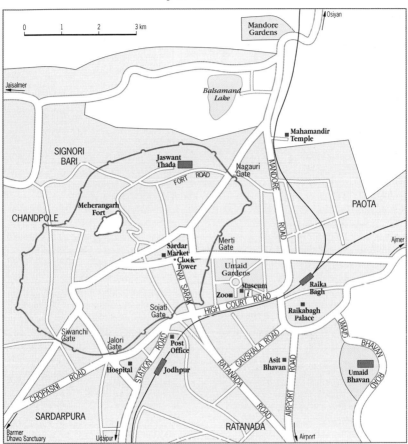

the British, with their merchant fleets, trade barriers and European goods, created a new maritime market. Jodhpur and Britain signed a treaty in 1818 and the canny Marwari merchants followed the trade, fanning out across India, where they have formed some of India's greatest industrial powerhouses. Little of their commercial influence can be seen here, but they retain links with their old homes. The city population is heading for a million, but it feels like a smaller town and has remarkably few facilities.

343km west of Jaipur and 602km from Delhi, with road, rail and air connections. Tourist Information Office, Hotel Ghoomar, High Court Road (tel: 45083).

Formidable Meherangarh towers over Jodhpur

JASWANT THADA

Just outside the fort is the modern royal cremation ground, centred on the huge marble monument (constructed in 1899) commemorating Maharaja Jaswant Singh II (1878–1895), a benevolent man who constructed schools and hospitals, roads and railways and is considered by most to be Jodhpur's finest ruler.

Opposite Meherangarh Fort, halfway up the hill. Open: daily, 9am–5pm. Admission free.

FAME AND FORTUNE

Jodhpur is, of course, most famous for its baggy riding trousers, introduced to the British cavalry during World War I by Maharaja Pratap Singh, while commander of the Mounted Lancers Regiment. Shortly afterwards, he lost his luggage during a sea voyage to England; he gave the tailor explicit instructions on how to make the trousers but the tailor needed a name to put in the order book. 'Jodhpuri', replied the Maharaja – and thus a fashion was born.

MEHERANGARH FORT

Founded in 1459 by Rao Jodha, this is one of the most dramatic palaces in Rajasthan – a towering fortress, high on a craggy 125m hill, with powerful walls 10km round and up to 45m high in places. As you walk up the steep, twisting path, designed to halt a charging elephant, through the seven monumental gateways, sheer cliffs of natural rock and smooth-cut stone of blood-red local sandstone soar to a frothy summit of lacy palace balconies. Several gateways are accompanied by memorials to people who died defending them and there are still cannon marks visible on the walls. Beside the last, the 15th-century **Loha Pol** (Iron Gate), are numerous *sati* handprints.

The palace, as it exists today, was only completed in 1853. It was divided in two, with the *zenana* (harem) to the left and the men's and public apartments to the right. Inside, it is rich with treasures. Rooms are lush with sandalwood, *faux bois*, real marble and marble effect, lacy *jali* screens, and painted panels and ceilings, reaching their most magnificent in the **Phool Mahal** (Flower Palace) with its gilded sandalwood ceiling that used 28kg of gold. Even better is the superb collection of furniture, which includes a richly inlaid stone table in the **Khabka Mahal**, several lavishly decorated royal cradles (one self-rocking, a gift from the local electricians' union) in the **Jhanki Mahal**, and a fantastic set of palanquins and elephant howdahs. There are also collections of miniature paintings in the **Umaid Vilas**, musical instruments and costumes in the **Ajit Vilas** and old manuscripts in the **Maharaja Mansingh Pushtak Prakash**. The arms collection includes the swords of Timur and Akbar, and there are even campaign tents used by Maharaja Abhai Singh, Shah Jahan and Aurangzeb.

Beyond the main palace buildings are the stables and guard rooms, a wide rampart and gun emplacements. The cannons were looted from Gujurat after the defeat of Ahmedabad in 1730. From the ramparts, there are stupendous views of the city. The prevalent pale blue traditionally marks the Brahmin houses, but its use has become more widespread because of its cooling and insect repellent properties (due to indigo in the paint). *4km from the city centre, up a very steep hill. Open: daily, 9am–5pm. Guided tours only within the palace. Admission and camera charge.*

A sumptuous collection of carriages, palanquins and howdahs still graces the fort

Sardar Market

SARDAR MARKET

At the centre of the old town, at the foot of the cliff, is one of the best bazaars in Rajasthan, where acres of covered stalls surround a huge open-air market selling a vast array of fruit and vegetables, spices and cooking pots, textiles and trinkets. This is not a particularly good place for souvenir shopping but the atmosphere is electric. The English Clock Tower was built by Maharaja Sardar Singh and completed in 1915.
Best visited in the morning or late afternoon. Open, free access.

UMAID BHAWAN

This stolid, imposing palace, designed by British architect, H V Lanchester, was the last and largest ever built. Conceived as a famine relief project, it was sited, on the advice of a holy man, on bedrock with no water supply. Between 1929 and 1943, 3,000 builders and craftsmen were employed to build the palace, blasting foundation trenches from the rock, to construct a road and a railway (in order to transport the materials), and to bore for water.

Members of the royal family still live upstairs and there is a small museum here, which contains a model and blueprints of the palace, model planes, and Jodhpuri history, art and crafts. The palace also now houses the city's most luxurious hotel.

Umaid Bhawan Road (tel: 33316).
Museum open: daily, 9am–5pm. Admission charge for all but residential guests.

UMAID GARDENS

At the centre of these green and shady gardens, laid out in 1909, with topiary elephants and camels, stands the somewhat moth-eaten **government museum**. It has some fine silver, enamel, porcelain, statuary and inlay work, but more interesting is the delightful toy collection, which includes ivory trains, cars, and elephants, lively models of people at work and crockery carved from rock salt. There is also the usual natural history section with displays of dead crocodiles, stuffed tigers in mortal combat and ageing things in pickling jars. There is a small zoo near by.

High Court Road. Museum (tel: 45353).
Open: 10am–4.30pm, closed Fridays.
Admission charge.

JODHPUR ENVIRONS

BALSAMAND SUMMER PALACE

First dammed in 1159 by Balak Rao Parihar, this delightful rainwater lake is a cool oasis amidst the rocky hills. The summer palace and gardens, heavy with mango trees, were laid out in 1936.

9km northeast of Jodhpur. Open: daily, 9am–6pm (palace closed to the public). Admission charge.

MANDORE

Inhabited since the late Gupta period (5th–6th century AD), Mandnaya-pura, the original capital of Marwar, once had a 10km wall and a population of 50,000. It was captured by the Rathores in 1381 and effectively abandoned when the court was transferred to Jodhpur in 1459. The ruins now stand in lush, shady gardens and are entered via the **Ajit Pol**, the gate that was built as a celebration of Ajit Singh's victory over the Moghuls in 1707.

Highlights of Mandore include: the graphic **Hall of Heroes**, a rock wall with high relief; brightly painted depictions of

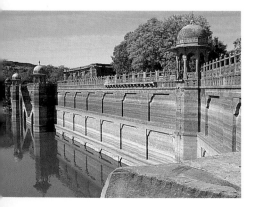

Balsamand Lake, playground of princes, is now a favourite local picnic spot

Lush gardens surround the ruins of Mandore, once capital of Marwar

local heroes such as Pabuji and Chamunda (1707–49); and the crowded modern **Shrine of 30 Crore (300 million) Gods**, among them Brahma, Lakshmi and Kali. The **Pleasure Palace of Abhai Singh** now encloses a small museum. Mandore remained the royal cremation ground and there are numerous memorial *chhatris* and temples, both Hindu and Jain, the earliest of which (on the hill) date from the 8th century. The finest are the memorials of Maharahas Jaswant Singh (1638–78) and Ajit Singh (1678–1731), the second of whom was cremated along with six queens and 58 concubines.
10km north of Jodhpur. Open access during daylight hours. Museum section open: 10am–4.30pm; closed Friday. Admission free.

OSIYAN

Osiyan was a major trading centre on the camel caravan routes during the Gupta period (3rd–6th century AD). It is now a small market town surrounded by sand dunes. Several 5th- to 11th-century temples, similar in style to those of South India, are still standing in three separate clusters. The largest of the Jain temples (dating from the 8th to the 10th centuries) is dedicated to Mahavira, with an idol made of milk and sand, covered in 400g of gold and said to be 2,500 years old. The ancient Chamunda temple near by (up 145 steps) is home to a statue said to have appeared magically out of the rock. Both statue and temple are drowned in tinsel and tin foil.
58km north of Jodhpur. Open, free access.

VILLAGE SAFARIS, see page 145.

MUD HUTS AND MILLET

The day begins at the household shrine, where every woman makes a quick offering to the gods. They also fetch the water, cook the meals, and look after the small children, then work with the men in the fields, growing millet and maize, chillies and vegetables. From about the age of five, the children join them, looking after chickens or cattle and helping with the harvest. Cattle and water buffalo are crucial to rural life, providing muscle power for ploughing, turning the irrigation wheels and producing milk. On the rare occasions when there is meat with the basic menu of vegetables and chapatis, it will almost certainly be goat. Rajasthan does have large flocks of sheep, however, and in the desert, where melons and bitter cucumbers sprawl out across the sand for only a few short weeks, the camel is king (see page 144). In their spare time, people weave, embroider or make pots. Some one-caste villages specialise as makers of toys or musical instruments, iron workers or saddlers.

Living close to the land and at the whim of the elements, nature is venerated and celebrated in a host of festivals marking the seasons, the harvests and the human rites of passage (see pages 158–9). Bright colours, whirling dances and noisy

The cities may be vast and impossibly crowded, but over 650 million people still live in villages across India, their life simple, hard-working and very poor but infinitely more pleasant than in the rat-infested city slums

instruments bring a gaiety to life that is only heightened during the local *mela*, a medieval-style market, stock market, fair and even religious festival crucial to the survival of isolated communities.

Nearly three-quarters of India's population still lives a traditional life of subsistence farming. Most villagers are poor. They live in simple thatched huts, sleep on rope *charpoys* or the floor, fetch water from communal wells and wash in a nearby river. Few have any education and medical facilities are patchy in the extreme. Nevertheless, most have just enough to eat and life, while hard, is rarely desperate.

Mount Abu

Mount Abu huddles among the rocks on a 1,220m granite table mountain at the far southwestern end of the Aravalli Hills. It was here that the Brahmins conducted the sacred rituals by fire which turned eager locals and victorious foreigners into Rajput warriors. From 1882 onwards, it became the head-quarters of the British Resident and the only hill station in Rajputana. British and Indian ruling classes alike flocked here to escape the ferocious heat of the plains. The government of Rajasthan still moves up here in May. Most of the summer palaces are now hotels, catering to a flood of Indian tourists, particularly honeymoon couples and pilgrims. There are hundreds of small temples in the vicinity, ranging from the ancient cave temple of Adhar Devi to the most recent a vast, pink Shiva *lingam* in the town centre. The surround-ing mountain jungle is a wildlife sanctuary with langur, sloth bear, wild boar, leopard, sambar and chinkara.

185km west of Udaipur and 326km southwest of Jodhpur, with good roads. The nearest rail station is Abu Road, 30km below, with bus and jeeps connecting. Tourist Information Office, opposite Bus Stand (tel: 3151).

ADHAR DEVI TEMPLE

This ancient temple is dedicated to the serpent goddess, Arbuda, patron of the town, who formed the mountain in order to save the sacred cow Nandi from drowning in an abyss. To reach the

temple, climb the 360 steps, squeeze through a narrow cleft between two massive rocks and enter the central cave temple on hands and knees, beneath a towering overhang. The black-painted marble idol, riding a solid gold tiger, is claimed to be about 5,000 years old.
2km north of town, off Subhash Road. Open, free access during daylight hours.

GOVERNMENT MUSEUM

A few interesting ceramics, glass plates and bronzes lurk, totally unlabelled, beneath the dust of the official government museum, surely one of the worst in Rajasthan.
Opposite Rajasthali, off Raj Bhavan Road. Open: 10am–5pm, closed Friday. Admission free.

NAKKI TALAV

The holiday centre of Mount Abu, this sparkling blue artificial lake is said to have been gouged from the earth by the gods, using their fingernails (*nakh* means nail). There are boats for hire, gardens,

Nakki Lake – popular with honeymooners

photographers with fancy tinsel costumes for you to dress up in, and souvenirs by the ton. Near by is the jazzed-up 14th-century Raghunath temple. Several massive boulders crowning the surrounding hills have been named. Toad Rock is the most obvious, but look also for the Nun, the Camel and Nandi (bull). *On the western edge of the town centre. Nakki Lake Road circles the entire lake. Open, free access. Rowing boats and pedaloes available for hire from the jetty by Gandhi Park.*

VIEW POINTS

Several points around the edge of the plateau offer spectacular views across the plains. The best are **Honeymoon Point** (Anadra Point) and **Sunset Point**, where hundreds of people gather to watch the sunset every evening in a carnival atmosphere of pony rides and souvenir sellers. **Baylay's Walk** is a pleasant 5km route from Nakki Lake to Sunset Point. *Honeymoon Point, 2.5km northwest on Ganesh Road; Sunset Point, 2km southwest on Sunset Point Road. Open, free access.*

MOUNT ABU

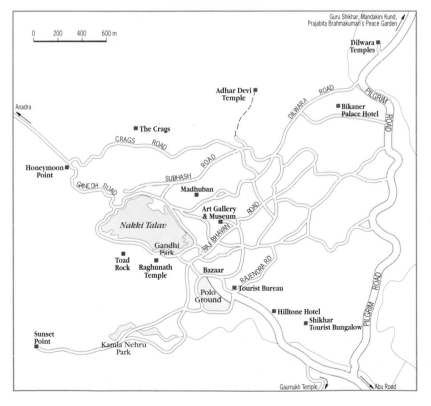

MOUNT ABU ENVIRONS

DILWARA TEMPLES

This complex of five marble Jain temples is one of the finest in Rajasthan, worth braving the queues and ferocious guards.

On the left as you enter is the relatively simple **Parshwanath Temple** (1458). Directly ahead is the earliest and most magnificent **Vimal Vasahi Temple**, built from 1031 by Vimal Shah, a Gujarati minister to King Bhim Devi I. He employed 1,500 artisans and 1,200 labourers for 14 years. Heralded by a column of white marble elephants, the cross-legged image of Adinath sits under a dome intricately sculpted with scenes from the lives of the gods. The large courtyard has 52 cells and a superb colonnade of rampantly joyful pillars. Up the steps, the spectacular **Luna Vasahi Temple** was built in 1231 by two brothers, Vastupal and Tajpal, both also Gujarati ministers. Dedicated to Neminath, it is similar in style to the Vimal Vasahi Temple, but if anything, the delicacy of the sculpture is even more perfect, culminating in a massive, central, many-layered lotus, carved from a single block. The **Pittalhar Temple** (Rishabh Deoji), built by Bhima Shah in 1489, has a huge brass statue of Adinath. The temple of **Mahaveer Swami** was added in 1582.

3.5km north of town, on Pilgrim Road. Open: daily, 12 noon–6pm for non-Jains. Admission free. Strictly no leather or photography (cameras not allowed inside).

GAUMUKH TEMPLE

Dedicated to Rama, this small temple (the Cow's Mouth) is centred on a spring gushing from the mouth of a marble cow. In the Hindu creation myth, the world is formed by a cow licking salt; the source of the Ganges has the same name. This is said to be the site of the ancient *agnikund* fire rituals.

4km south of Mount Abu. Open, free access, down 700 very steep steps.

GURU SHIKHAR

At 1,722m, this is the highest peak between the Himalayas and the southern Nilgiri Hills. On the summit are a radar station and a temple, the latter dedicated to Guru Dattatreya (an incarnation of Vishnu) and reached by 367 steps.

16km north of Mount Abu. Open access (except to the radar station).

MANDAKINI KUND

Sitting on a site held sacred for 5,000 years, the Achaleshwar Mahadeo has a small hole plummeting deep into the earth in place of the usual *lingam*. It was created by Shiva, who stamped hard to quieten the earthquakes plaguing the area, and no one has ever managed to measure its true depth. In the side is a small, rounded rock, said to be Lord Shiva's toe.

The stepped **Mandakini Kund** was the water supply for **Achalgarh** fort, built on a nearby hill by the 15th-century Mewari ruler, Rana Kumbha. Beside the tank are lifesize

ATTENTION PLEASE.
RULES FOR ENTRY IN TEMPLES
- ENTRY: FREE.
- VISITING HOURS 12ɴɴ TO 6ᴘ.ᴍ.(MORNING HOURS RESERVED FOR POOJA,WORSHIP FOR JAINS.
- PERSONAL ARTICLES LIKE BAGS,SHOES,UMBRELLAS,FIRE-ARMS,EATABLES,DRINKABLES,ALL TYPES OF LEATHER-ARTICLES,RADIO,TRANSISTOR,CAMERA ᴇᴛᴄ.NOT ALLOWED.
- NONE SHALL ENTER THE TEMPLE WITH BETEL OR ANY KIND OF EATABLES IN THE MOUTH. KINDLY THROW-OUT
- WASH THE MOUTH. SMOKING IS PROHIBITED.
- DO NOT TOUCH PIECES OF ART· SCULPTURES WITH YOUR HAND .ANY PART ᴏꜰ BODY OR ANY OTHER THING .
- DO NOT ENTER ANY OF THE CELLS WHERE JAINS IDOLS,GODS· GODESSES ARE ENSHRINED .
- SECURITY STAFF HAS RIGHT TO CHECK THE VANITY BAGS ᴸ BELONGINGS OF ANY BODY AT ENTRANCE OR ANY TIME WHILE IN TEMPLE.
- IN TEMPLE CAMPUS, MOVING WITH HAND-IN-HAND, HAND ON SHOULDIER OR WAISTE IS STRICTLY PROHIBITED.
- KINDLY OBSERVE ABOVE RULES ᴸ INSTRUCTIONS GIVEN BY THE TEMPLE PERSONNEL ON DUTY TO MAINTAIN ᴸ PRESERVE THE SANCTITY AND SACREDNESS OF THE TEMPLES.
— CHET KARKARA.

Jain pilgrims flock to the magnificent Dilwara Temples

statues of three buffaloes and the Parmar king Adipal. According to legend, in ancient times it was filled with ghee (melted butter). Each night, three demon buffaloes would sneak down and drink it dry. Eventually the sages went to King Adipal, who cornered the demons and shot all three with one arrow.

11km north of Mount Abu on the Guru Shikar road. Open, free access.

PRAJABITA BRAHMAKUMARI'S PEACE GARDEN

In 1984 the Brahma Kumari sect created this garden of flags and poinsettias to promote peace and harmony. The sect's Mount Abu headquarters includes a spiritual museum and university.

8km north of Mount Abu, on the road to Guru Shikar. Open: daily, 10am–noon and 2.30–5pm. Admission free.

Ranthambore

FORT

Built in AD944 by a Chauhan ruler, Ranthambore stands at the gateway between the Moghul north and central India. As a result, it became a political football, with control swinging backwards and forwards between Delhi and the Rajputs. Only one great tragedy is recorded by legend. In 1301, as Ala-ud-Din Khalji laid siege, Prince Hammir and his warriors went out to fight, telling the ladies of the court to commit *johar* should they lose sight of the standard. The Rajputs won, chasing the Sultan's troops into the distance. As the standard vanished, the ladies committed *johar* and Hamir's triumphant return was greeted by their bodies. He was so appalled that he too committed suicide. In 1569 Ranthambore was eventually defeated by Akbar, who handed it to the Maharaja of Amber (Jaipur), ending its history as an independent kingdom.

The seven gates and massive curtain walls, crowning a flat-topped, 225m hill with sheer sides and dramatic views, are still intact and forbidding. Near the entrance is Hamir's badly damaged but romantic palace (12th- to 13th-century), with mirrored rooms, fountains and balconies overlooking the plain. There are also several water tanks and temples, of which the most important is an undistinguished 10th-century temple to Ganesh, now a popular place of pilgrimage. Those who visit leave the god reminders of their prayers; their old rags if they have asked for new clothes, a little heap of stones representing a new house. He even gets thousands of wedding invitations a year.

NATIONAL PARK

Used as a hunting ground by the Maharaja of Jaipur, Ranthambore became a game sanctuary in 1955 and one of the original nine Project Tiger reserves in 1972 (see pages 122–3). The core area of 274sq km became a National Park in 1980, and in 1992 the bordering Keladevi and Man Singh sanctuaries were added, with wildlife 'corridors' running between the protected areas. The total protected area now covers

Sambar wallow in Ranthambore Lake, numbers rising rapidly in the safety of the national park

Ranthambore's jungle-clad hills are one of the last havens of the tiger

1,334sq km, of which only a tiny portion is open to the public.

Officially, there are about 25 tigers in the national park and another 11 in Keladevi. It is possible to see them here, but it requires patience and luck. They are extremely solitary creatures, covering a wide territory, and are so well camouflaged that they fade into the thick undergrowth literally yards from the road.

Tigers or not, Ranthambore has magic. Cavernous banyan trees drip roots, while the skinny twisted dhok trees scramble across the hills, turning flaming red in autumn. If tigers are rare, numerous other species are very visible. You will certainly see the antelopes – nilgai, sambar and chittal – and the lucky ones may also find sloth bears, wild boar, chinkara, caracal, porcupines and jackals (see pages 142–3). The lakes are filled with lotus and crocodiles, and 264 species of bird have been recorded. And if that were not enough, the whole area is littered with ruined pavilions and *chhatris*, the finest of which is the Jogi Mahal, the old guest house by the lake.

Ranthambore is 14km from Sawai Madhopur, the nearest town and station; 157km from Jaipur and 361km from Delhi. Tourist information, tours by jeep or lorry bookable at the Project Tiger Office, Sawai Madhopur (tel: 20223), open 10am–5pm. Fort – entrance beside the park gate; open access during daylight hours. Admission free. National Park open: daily, 6.30–10am and 2–5.30pm (closed 1 July–30 September). You will be accompanied by a guide and must stick to the allocated route. Entry is relatively expensive, with separate fees for entrance, vehicle hire, guide and camera charges.

PROJECT TIGER

By 1973 the world population of tigers was down to around 3,600, about 1,800 of them in India. Project Tiger was born out of a last ditch effort to save them from extinction. There are now 19 nature reserves within the scheme, two of them, Ranthambore and Sariska, in Rajasthan. All humans were moved out of the park areas which were then fenced off. Each is now surrounded by a buffer zone where people can graze cattle and collect wood, but not live or farm. Locals are

TIGER TIGER BURNING BRIGHT

Largest of the great cats, weighing up to 200kg, the tiger is remarkably versatile, surviving in a variety of habitats and climates, and able to swim and climb trees. They do need space, however; a single male will have a territory of up to 100sq km, which he will share with 3 to 5 females, each of whom may have 3 to 6 cubs. The cubs stay with the mother until about the age of two and a half. Tigers stalk, rather than chase, grabbing the prey from behind and killing it swiftly. Ideally, they look for a large animal which will last them four or five days. Once adult, their only predators are human, many of whom still sadly believe that the skins look better on a wall, and that eating powdered bones will increase their courage and sexual prowess.

compensated for the loss of land and any stock or crops destroyed by wild animals. They are also being helped to find alternative sources of income.

The scheme has succeeded, to some extent, and the difference between the lush vegetation inside and the eroded craters outside the perimeter fences is staggering. India now claims a tiger population of around 3,000 (sadly down from a high of around 4,500). Project Tiger's very success has

attracted back the poachers and tigers are once more fighting for survival against the Chinese medicine men. Game wardens talk nervously about parks being for all species, not just tigers. They seem to be preparing the world for the day, potentially within the next few years, when they are obliged to admit that the tiger is extinct in the wild.

Udaipur

*I*n 1536 Banbir, a pretender to the throne of Mewar, assassinated the Maharana and then went in search of his baby brother, Udai Singh. Word reached the nursery just in time and the young prince's nurse, Panna Bai, switched the baby with her own. A few minutes later she watched helplessly as her own baby was disembowelled by the traitor. The grieving mother then smuggled Udai Singh out of Chittorgarh to Kumbhalgarh, where he grew up under the protection of the governor – the same man who would eventually help him regain his throne when he was 15. In 1557 Udai Singh was out hunting in the Aravalli Hills when he came across a holy man who told him to establish a new city on the very spot where they had met, prophesying that it would never be defeated in battle.

UDAIPUR

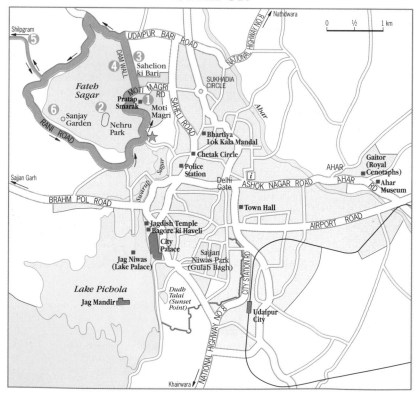

Monumental arches lead to the bathing *ghats*

Within two years graceful Udaipur was born, with a 10km-long wall and 11 gates – of which five survive. Mewar was the only Rajput state never to accept Moghul domination. Today, with a population of some 350,000, it is a peaceful place, 700m above sea level, with buildings of white and cream mirrored in expanses of deep-blue water.

374km from Jaipur; good road, rail and air connections. Tourist Information Office, RTDC Hotel Kajri, Shastri Circle, Udaipur (tel: 29535).

BAGORE KI HAVELI

This 18th-century house on the banks of Lake Pichola was built by a minor rajah. It served as a royal guest house for a number of years and now houses the **Western Zone Cultural Centre**, which demonstrates crafts from Rajasthan, Gujarat, Goa and Maharashtra, and has a small museum. The archway next door leads down to the **Gangaur Ghat**, where men and women gather in separate sections to bathe and do their laundry. The *ghats* are lined by numerous small shrines.

Lake Pichola (tel: 23858). Open: 10am–5pm, closed Sunday. Admission free. Open access to the bathing ghats *(strictly no photographs).*

CITY PALACE

The largest palace complex in Rajasthan is in fact a series of several palaces, large and small, tacked on by successive Maharanas over 400 years, with such success that they run together seamlessly.

About half of the complex (to the right) is still the private residence of the royal family. On the left are two hotels; the very grand **Shiv Niwas** (stop for a drink or tea to look around) and the less opulent **Fateh Prakash Palace**. The lavishly decorated central portion is open to the public.

Built in 1725, the triple-arched **Tripolia Pol** leads through to the massive **Bada Chowk** (outer courtyard), large enough to house the massed army of Mewar, including 100 elephants. It used to be the custom for the Maharajah to be weighed under the arches, and his weight in gold distributed to the poor. Near the entrance to the **government museum**, with its *memorabilia* of Rana Pratap Singh, is a family tree, dating back to 566. For the last 200 years, all the Maharanas were adopted (from within the Sisodia family) as a curse gave them only daughters. The last Maharana eventually had two sons, but only after he had lost his title.

The interior of the palace winds through a long series of rooms, some very plain, others enormously decorative, with workmanship and taste ranging from the sublime to the ridiculous. The 300-year-old **Bada Mahal** appears to have a terraced garden and bathing pool on the 4th floor; in fact, it is a hill which was cut away as the palace was built around it. The **Dilkhush Mahal** (Jovial Palace, 1620–80) has a series of magnificent miniature frescos. Even better are those in the entrancingly decorated **Krishna Mahal**, now a memorial to a 16-year-old princess who, in the 19th century, committed suicide rather than risk war between two rival suitors.

Beyond this is the oriental **Manek**

Technicolour glass in the City Palace, Udaipur

Mahal (Ruby Palace), in which the 18th-century **Chini Chitrashala** is decorated in blue and white Chinese tiles, swapped for opium (a major local industry). The upper storeys formed the *zenana* (harem), now housing the museum collection, including silver and gold ornaments and miniature paintings. Several rooms are elaborately decorated with paintings, coloured glass and tiles, and culminate in the gaudy **Queen's Make-up Room**, which boasts a one-way mirror that allowed the Maharana to watch the queen unobserved.

Downstairs, the **Mor Chowk** (Peacock Courtyard) takes its name from three mosaic peacocks representing the seasons. Just off the courtyard are the public apartments with an almost psychedelic dining room, lined with glass tiles, surrounding a huge 19th-century representation of the Sun God.

Lake Pichola (tel: 23201). Open: daily, 9.30am–4.30pm. Admission and photo charge. Separate fee for the museum.

Above: the towering canopies of the City Palace
Below: locals bathe and do their laundry in Lake Pichola

The Lake Palace is now one of India's most romantic and luxurious hotels

JAGDISH TEMPLE

Approached by steep steps guarded by stone elephants and carved all over with jolly dancing girls, this temple was built by Maharana Jagat Singh I in 1651. Inside are a massive black stone idol of Vishnu as Jagannath, Lord of the Universe, and a bronze statue of the eagle, Garuda.
Beside the City Palace. Open access.

LAKE FATEH SAGAR, see pages 134–5.

LAKE PICHOLA

First built in the 14th century, Lake Pichola was strengthened and enlarged by Maharana Udai Singh while he was building the city in the 16th century, and now covers about 8sq km. It is fed only by rainwater and in times of severe drought has dried up completely.

Dudh Talai Park

At the top of this small hillside park, Sunset Point, with its cafés, street vendors and children's playground, provides the city's best view of the sunset over Lake Pichola.

Jag Niwas (Lake Palace)

Built as a summer palace in 1746 by Maharana Jagat Singh II, this is a romantic fairy-tale confection of delicate white marble skimming the surface of the lake. It shot to fame, courtesy of James Bond, as the island home of *Octopussy*, and has become one of the classic images of Rajasthan. Since 1962 it has been the luxurious Lake Palace Hotel.

Jag Mandir

Built on a sandstone base and surrounded by splendid carved elephants, this small island palace was

GAITOR

The memorial *chhatris* of the royal Sisodia family are clustered in an overgrown garden. The oldest tombs, furthest from the gate, were built of lime-covered brick, while later additions were of marble. The two massive temple-like structures belong to Maharanas Amar Singh (1698–1710) and Sangram Singh (1710–34), both of whom were noted for their bravery against the Moghuls.
*Ahar Road, 4km from Lake Pichola. The gates are locked, but the doorkeeper will admit you at any time. Admission free (*baksheesh *required).*

founded by Maharana Karan Singh as a royal guesthouse and takes its name from Jagat Singh I, who completed the work. In 1623 the Moghul Prince Khurram (later to take the throne as Shah Jahan) rebelled against his father and took refuge here.

Boat tours round the lake and to the Jag Mandir leave from the Lake Palace jetty beside the City Palace. Only guests or diners are allowed inside the Lake Palace.

UDAIPUR MUSEUMS

Ahar
The small dusty archaeological site of Dhum Kot produced a fascinating record of life in the area as far back as 4,000BC, but like most digs it is somewhat underwhelming to look at. Beside it is a small archaeological museum with numerous pre-Aryan exhibits, including some stunning Copper Age pots and later temple statuary, found at this and other nearby sites.
Ahar Road, 4km from Lake Pichola (no tel). Open: 10am–4.30pm; closed Friday. Admission free.

Bhartiya Lok Kala Mandal (Folklore Museum)
This is a delightful if sadly dusty folk museum, stuffed full of entertaining treasures. It is very much a working museum with craft workshops, an academic wing gathering recordings of folk tales and music, and its own highly acclaimed dance and puppet troops. Among the exhibits are displays on turban tying, decorative henna patterns on hands, village shrines, *pads*, *pichwai* and *kavads* (see pages 130–1), and puppets. The curator is happy to talk for hours about local crafts and traditions.

Chetak Circle (tel: 24296). Open: daily, 9am–6pm, with performances 6–7pm. Admission charge.

Sajjan Niwas Park
This lush park, with a splendid rose garden (the **Gulab Bagh**) laid out by Maharana Sajjan Singh (1874–84), has a small zoo and a 2km toy train track.
Lake Palace Road. Open: daily, 10am–5pm.

Sahelion ki Bari and Shilpgram, see pages 134–5.

Shah Jahan once lived on the little island of Jag Mandir, a temple to Rajput hospitality

PERFECTION IN MINIATURE

Surviving Hindu paintings stretch back to at least the 14th century. The earliest examples were painted on banana and palm leaf, but beside them lay a host of other media including frescoes, scroll paintings known as *pichwai* (hung in temples) or *pads* (used in telling folk tales), and little wooden travelling *kavads* (box theatres/temples painted like strip cartoons). Most concentrated on religious themes and were designed to tell a story inspired by epic tales, such as the *Ramayana* and *Gita Govindha*, and by *Ragas* (musical mood poems). The paintings were bold and brightly coloured, rich with natural life and, in many cases, a natural eroticism.

Islamic art grew out of the production of illustrated manuscripts. Painting in the more formal, softly coloured Persian style was introduced to India by Emperor Humayun, who brought back two artists on his return from exile in 1556. With a religion that disapproved of iconography, the Moghul painters were strictly secular, creating riotous scenes of feasts and hunts, tender love stories and stately processions. Akbar, ever curious and illiterate throughout his life, began to hire Indian artists to illustrate Hindu texts for him to study. Inevitably, the two styles began to merge.

Ironically, it was the puritanical Aurangzeb who prompted the final stage of evolution. He disapproved of frivolity and was determined to stamp out what he saw as idolatry. The painters fled his court, many of them

seeking shelter with the Rajput princes, taking their Persian-influenced Moghul style back into Hindu art. The brushes of individual artists also helped to shape distinctive regional schools of painting that still exist today, from the elegant minutiae of courtly Udaipur to the sketchier, bolder freedom of Jodhpur. Today, tiny, delicate miniature paintings of traditional themes are still produced on paper and silk as they have been for 300 years.

Modern artists still use the same techniques followed by Persian, Moghul and Rajput miniature painters

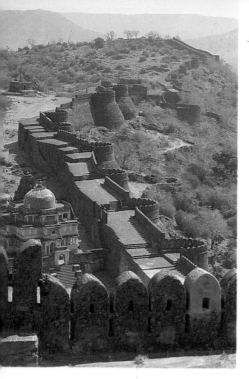

Rambling hilltop Kumbhalgarh was the last refuge of countless Mewar kings

buildings at Chittorgarh (see pages 78–9), and became a place of safety for the royal family. Udai Singh was brought up and crowned here after his escape from treachery (see page 124). It was sacked only once, by the combined armies of the Moghuls, Amber and Marwar.

A 36km-long outer curtain wall encloses an inner fort area of over 12sq km, with a steep approach through seven massive gateways. The fort had everything it needed to withstand a lengthy siege, including fields, water and kitchen gardens. There are even said to have been 365 temples. A village still thrives in the outer courtyard. The main palace building, the **Badal Mahal** (Cloud Palace), occupies the highest point of the hill, approached by another very steep and winding footpath. Several rooms still have fine wall paintings, but the real stars are the superb panoramic views and the sheer drama of the setting.

A 578sq km area in the surrounding hills has been declared a **wildlife sanctuary**. Among other species, it is home to leopards, chinkara, sloth bear, porcupines and flying squirrels, and is the only successful breeding ground of wolves in India. There are several good hiking trails through the jungle.
*84km north of Udaipur. Open access during daylight hours. The palace keys are held by a guide (*baksheesh *required).*

UDAIPUR ENVIRONS

AMBIKA MATA TEMPLE
This ancient and venerated temple is a popular place of pilgrimage. It was built in AD960 and dedicated to the goddess, Durga, the goddess of war, in her many incarnations. It has particularly fine and sensual carvings of celestial nymphs and beautiful women.
Jagat, 50km southeast of Udaipur. Open access.

JAISAMAND, see page 140.

KUMBHALGARH
The second most important fort in Mewar, this is another magnificent mountain ruin, sprawled massively across the hills at an altitude of 1,087m. It was built in 1458 by Rana Kumbha, who was also responsible for some of the finest

RANAKPUR
Set in a peaceful, wooded river valley, this complex of Jain temples is the largest and one of the most holy in Rajasthan. It is hugely popular with pilgrims, and has three dormitory hostels and a massive

dining room to prove it. From the tourist's point of view, it also includes some of the most astonishingly beautiful temple carving in the whole of India.

The complex was founded in the mid-14th century, but most of the buildings date from the 15th. The smaller, outlying temples are relatively simple. The highlight is the **Chaumukha Temple**, a huge walled complex covering 3,600sq m, on a high stone plinth, approached by steep steps. Inside are a staggering 29 halls and 1,444 pillars. Carved from a creamy white marble, made translucent by the sunshine, each pillar is different, finer and more intricate than the last. An extraordinary imagination has created images of goddesses and nymphs, dancers and elephants, scenes of daily life and glorious fantasy that soar far beyond the mundane. Access to the roof leads to a whole new world of elaborate domes, spires and prayer flags. At the centre is a huge, four-faced idol of Adinath, Giver of Truth.

95km north of Udaipur on the Jodhpur Road. Open: to visitors, 11am–5pm. Admission free, but photo charge. Strictly no leather or photos of the idols (also read the amazingly detailed list of prohibitions by the main office).

SAJJAN GARH (Monsoon Palace)
Built by Maharana Sajjan Singh in the late 18th century, this little palace is perched high on a steep hill, overlooking Lake Pichola. The views of the city are superb, but the palace itself is closed.
About 15km from the city, up very steep, poorly maintained hairpin bends. Allow about 3 hours for the round trip.

No two pillars are the same at Ranakpur Temple

The Upper Lakes

This tour covers the entire 9km circumference of green and tranquil Fateh Sagar. A good alternative is to walk the east shore. For the main route, see the Udaipur town plan on page 124. *Allow 3 hours.*

Start beside the bridge linking the Fateh Sagar and smaller Swaroop Sagar. Follow the lakeshore road north to the entrance of Moti Magri Park.

1 PRATAP SMARAK

Moti Magri (Pearl Hill) was the site of the first city of Udaipur, although only a few fragmentary walls mark the spot. The steep hill is now a lavish garden with wonderful views. At the top, the Pratap Smarak is a monument to Maharana Pratap Singh, the only Rajput ruler never to submit to the Moghuls, with a splendid equestrian bronze of the gallant Maharana riding his favourite horse, Chetak (see page 136). There are also a bird garden and small museum.

Turn right out of the entrance, and follow the road past the souvenir and drinks stands to the boat hire area and jetty. From here ferries run regularly to Nehru Park. There are also pedaloes, rowing boats and canoes for hire.

BATTLE OF HALDIGHATI

> **PRATAP SINGH**
>
> Son of Udai Singh, the founder of Udaipur, Pratap Singh is one of the greatest heroes of Rajasthan. Succeeding his father in 1572, at the height of the conflict with Akbar, he swore never to submit to the Moghul Emperor, or to sleep in his own bed until Mewar was safe. Taking to the hills with a band of followers, he waged war for 25 years. At his death in 1597, Mewar was still free.

2 NEHRU PARK

Work on this attractive island began in 1937 under the auspices of Maharana Bhupal Singh, who intended to build a water palace as a famine relief project. The palace was never completed and after Independence the island was turned into a public garden, named after Prime Minister Jawaharlal Nehru.

Continue round the lake. A road to the right, round the back of Moti Magri, leads to the Sahelion ki Bari.

3 SAHELION KI BARI (GARDEN OF THE MAIDS OF HONOUR)

Built by Maharana Sangram Singh (1710–34) for his 10 daughters, this is one of the most beautiful water gardens in Rajasthan. It is filled with delights such as the Rain without Cloud Fountain (listen to the sound) and the elaborate lily-filled Sekuntala Fountain, named after the eldest daughter. Jets of water shooting from the elephants' trunks were designed to create rainbows.

Return to the lakeshore road and cross the dam wall.

4 DAM WALL

Fateh Sagar was originally constructed in 1678 but its dam was washed away by heavy floods. The elegant dam wall with its string of small pavilions was rebuilt in 1889 by Maharana Fateh Singh, after whom the lake is now named.

The road turns back along the western shore. Towards the end, a well-signed turning to the right leads to the Shilpgram.

5 SHILPGRAM

Founded in 1989, this delightful arts and crafts complex has a small, beautifully

Small rural life museum at Shilpgram

designed museum with costumes, headgear and shoes, kitchen utensils, musical instruments, toys and ornaments, and a complex of authentic village dwellings from Rajasthan, Gujarat, Goa and Maharashtra, built by local people out of traditional materials. Musicians, dancers, puppeteers and acrobats regularly perform in the outdoor arena.

Return to the lakeshore road and follow it back to your starting point. Halfway along the south shore is the Sanjay Garden.

6 SANJAY GARDEN

Another tiny island garden, with a splendid multi-coloured fountain, this was named after Indira Gandhi's eldest son, Sanjay, who was killed in a flying accident.

Pratap Sanak, Moti Magri Hill (tel: 26010). Open: 7am–7pm. Admission charge (plus extra for vehicles).
The **Sahelion ki Bari**, Moti Magri Road, and the **Shilpgram**, Fateh Sagar Rani Road (tel: 86034). Both open: daily, 9am–6pm. Admission charge.

North from Udaipur

This drive through the Aravalli hills offers a delightful glimpse of rural Rajasthan and visits two magnificent sights, Kumbhalgarh and Ranakpur. *Allow one very long day; preferably two.*

Leave Udaipur on the NH8, heading north aross the hills to Kailashpur.

1 EKLINGJI TEMPLE

This famous complex of 108 temples in Kailashpur village was first built in AD734 and then rebuilt by Maharana Raimal (1473–1509). Dedicated to Shiva, it includes an ornate, pyramid-roofed pillared hall, a four-faced black marble image of Shiva and the only known Lalkulish temple in India (AD971). At nearby **Nagda**, a 15th-century Adbhutji Jain temple and two 11th-century Vishnu temples stand near a small lake.

Continue north through a rocky gorge along the NH8. After about 12km, a turning to the left leads 5km to the Haldi Ghati battlefield.

2 HALDI GHATI

This is the site of Pratap Singh's most famous battle, on 21 June 1576. The Maharana came face to face with Man Singh of Jaipur, leader of the Moghul army, mounted on an elephant. Pratap's pure white horse, Chetak, leapt up to strike the elephant which fled after badly wounding Chetak and Pratap Singh. The valiant horse leapt a stream to carry his master to safety before dying and is revered as a true hero of Mewar, with a monument near by. There is little to see here.

Return to the main road and continue

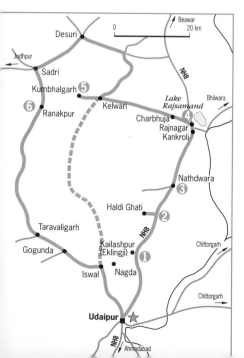

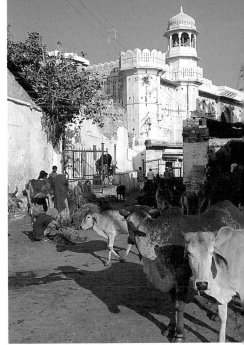
Cows wander freely in downtown Nathdwara

northwards for another 8km to Nathdwara. Turn left past the bus station, park and walk through the bazaar to the temple.

3 NATHDWARA TEMPLES
In 1669 followers of the Vallabhachari sect fled from Mathura and Aurangzeb's tyranny with a sacred black idol of Lord Krishna. At Nathdwara, the wheels of their chariot sank and taking it as a sign, they stopped and built a temple to house the image. Today the temple is popular among Hindu pilgrims. Eight times daily a new *pichwai* (painted cloth telling the life of Krishna) is hung behind the statue. It is difficult for non-Hindus to get inside, but the buzzing bazaar is well worth a stop.

Return to the main road and continue north, following signs for Ajmer. Just beyond Kankroli, home of the Vaishna Dwarikadheesh Temple, is the lake.

4 LAKE RAJSAMAND
Lined by marble pavilions and *chhatris*, this pleasant lake was built in 1660 by Maharana Raj Singh. Maharani Charumati built the Nauchowki Pavilion to honour her husband, Raj Singh I, who married her to save her from Aurangzeb. Other fine buildings include a palace and garden built by the 19th-century Maharana, Sajjan Singh, and the beautifully carved home of the Jain prime minister, Dayal Shah.

The road now runs through massive marble works to Khomsi, where you turn left for Charbhuja, which has another popular Vaishna pilgrimage temple, and Kelwari. From here, it is 9km up a steep mountain road to Kumbhalgarh. There is also a road back to Udaipur.

5 KUMBHALGARH
See page 132.

Go back down the hill to Saira and turn right for Ranakpur, 20km further on.

6 RANAKPUR JAIN TEMPLES
See pages 132–3.

It is 95km back to Udaipur, via Gogunda and Iswal.

Eklingi Temple, Kailashpur, 22km from Udaipur. Open: daily, 5–7am, 10am–1pm and 5–7pm. Inner sanctum closed to non-Hindus.
Nagda Temples, open access during daylight hours.
Nathdwara Temple, open 12 noon–1pm for non-Hindus (theoretically).

EACH IN HIS RIGHTFUL PLACE

Caste is at the heart of Indian culture, a rigid framework which slots every Hindu into an immediately recognisable category. You are born into a caste and can never change it. Education, career and financial advancement need not depend on caste but it is rare to find low caste people in high office and you would never find a high caste person sweeping the streets. Many don't even try to improve their lot, believing that their low status is *karma* (fate), a punishment for misdeeds in a former life. According to religious law, you cannot marry into a different caste – although this is easing to some extent in the cities. Non-Hindus do not have a caste system. In practice, an unofficial system has grown up to create definite class structures among all Indians.

There are four main caste groupings, each of them split into a multitude of sub-castes, according to occupation, area and so on. The three Aryan castes are considered to be 'twice-born' – old souls who are infinitely superior human beings. The priestly **Brahmins**, responsible for fixing the system in stone, are the highest caste. Theoretically, they do not have secular power, but they are responsible for the spiritual life of the people and act as king-makers. Many have also amassed a good deal of earthly wealth and authority. The secular rulers, soldiers and administrators belong to the **Kshatriya** (warrior) caste. In Rajasthan they are known as Rajputs. The **Vaishyas** are the cultivators.

At the bottom of the heap are the **shudras** (untouchables) who traditionally handle all the dirty jobs, from slaughtering animals to disposing of sewage. The doctrine of untouchability was created by orthodox Brahmins who felt that their spiritual purity would be polluted if they were touched by even the shadow of a *shudra*. Until recently, untouchables were not even allowed into the temples. Gandhi was the first to challenge the system, calling them the Harijan (Children of God). Untouchability is now banned by the constitution, and a percentage of all government jobs are reserved for the Scheduled Castes, as they are known. They themselves prefer the name **Dalit** (the Oppressed).

GETTING AWAY FROM IT ALL

'The villages are more pictorially
beautiful and more alien than
anything I had ever imagined.
The country people… are of
extraordinary personal beauty.
Their clothes are the only colour
in a nearly burnt-up land.
And what colour!'

ROBERT LUTYENS,
letter to his mother, 3 November 1937

NATIONAL PARKS

DESERT NATIONAL PARK

In 1972, a massive 3,162sq km of the Thar Desert was designated a national park, ironically in order to preserve it from irrigation schemes (see page 11). There are 27 villages located within the park, and several areas such as the Sam Dunes and Akal Fossil Park are now open to tourists. The 300sq km core is dedicated to scientific study, and special permits are required to gain access to it. Animal life within the park includes chinkara, desert fox, desert cat, desert hare and lizards. This is also a breeding ground for the rare great Indian bustard, and a winter retreat for many birds, including sparrows, imperial sand grouse, demoiselle cranes, lesser bustard, and numerous raptors including eagles, falcons and harriers.

30km from Jaisalmer (285km from Jodhpur). Permission from the District Magistrate, Collector's Office, Jaisalmer, near the Tourist Bungalow (tel: 2201). See also page 104.

JAISAMAND

This large and astonishingly beautiful lake, which extends over 160sq km and is ringed by gentle hills, was dammed by Maharana Jai Singh in 1685. Two royal summer palaces, the Hawa Mahal and the Roothi Rani Ka Mahal, overlook the lake, while the dam wall is topped by marble *chhatris*, decorated with finely carved elephants, and a small Shiva temple. Near the lake, a 52sq km wildlife sanctuary is the home of a wide variety of birds, as well as chittal, chinkara, wild boar and leopard. The surrounding area is the Bheel tribal homeland.

48km south of Udaipur. Open access.

KEOLADEO GHANA BIRD SANCTUARY

One of the world's great sanctuaries, these 29sq km of marsh and savannah provide a home to a staggering 360 species of bird. It is a magnet for bird watchers, but also a haven of peace in which to escape urban India. Among the bulbuls, doves, egrets, and ducks are seven species of birds of prey, several species of heron, stork, and owl and a migrant population of rare Siberian cranes. Land animals include chittal, sambar, nilgai, blackbuck, jungle cats and pythons.

Qualified naturalists are available as tour guides (ask at the gate) and most rickshaw wallahs are also knowledgeable. No motorised transport inside, either walk, hire a bicycle or use a cycle rickshaw (standard hourly rate). In season, rowing boats are available for marsh tours. Breeding season is August to October; the migrants arrive October to late February. Best viewing times, early morning and late afternoon. See also page 70.

Left: sambar deer buck feeding
Opposite: Indian wild boar

KUMBHALGARH SANCTUARY,
See page 132.

RANTHAMBORE, see pages 120–1.

SARISKA

Once a royal hunting ground, since 1979,
Sariska has been a Project Tiger reserve
(see pages 122–3), consisting of a 72sq
km National Park, surrounded by an
800sq km wildlife sanctuary. Set in the
rocky Aravalli Hills, it is a lovely
wilderness of tangled woodlands and
steep hills, interspersed by open
savannah, lakes and waterholes. The
animal population is large, with,
supposedly, 500 hyenas, 32 leopards and
24 tigers, as well as jungle cats, foxes,
jackals, wildboar, and plentiful sambar,
chittal and nilgai. There is also a thriving
bird population. Unfortunately, access
has now been restricted to one drive and
the undergrowth is so dense that it can be
extremely difficult to spot anything more
than a few yards from the road.
37km southwest of Alwar on the Jaipur road.
Open: daily, 6.30–10am and 2–5.30pm;
closed 1 July to 30 September. You will be
accompanied by a guide and must stick to the
route. Admission charges per person, vehicle
and camera, plus jeep hire.

A golden jackal takes a rest but stays alert

**MINOR PARKS AND
SANCTUARIES**
Bhensrod Garh Sanctuary, 53km
from Kota.
Darrah Sanctuary, 50km from Kota.
Dhawa (Doli) Sanctuary, 45km from
Jodhpur.
Gajner Sanctuary, 35km from
Bikaner.
Sitamata Sanctuary, 200km from
Udaipur.
Tal Chapper Sanctuary, 200km
from Jaipur.

FLORA AND FAUNA

Often overshadowed by the cities, the architecture and the sheer press of people, India has a rich and varied natural world. Even in the cities, regiments of spiky ashok trees line formal gardens; the peepul, sacred since it shaded Buddha during his Enlightenment, is still used for shade and as medicine; while the glossy, rounded mango tree, staple of royal orchards, is still generous, its fruit, flowers and bark used to eat, as perfume and for dyes. Out of town, the twisted hardwood dhok, whose leaves flame in autumn, carpets the Aravalli Hills, while the thorny acacia dominates the desert. For a few short weeks after the rains each year, the dunes glow with a million luminous yellow tennis balls, a melon-type creeping fruit known as the camel fruit

or desert apple. Finest of all is the superb, pendulous banyan, with roots flowing earthwards from its massive branches.

In the national parks, chittal, with chestnut coats liberally spotted in white and branched antlers, daintily browse in the dappled woodland. The larger nilgai (blue bulls), with a blue-grey sheen on its heavy body, splash through the marshland, and in an open, grassy clearing is a herd of buff brown sambar, the male's antlers resplendent as the *Monarch of the Glen*. Far away, on the fringes of the desert, grazes India's only gazelle, the chinkara.

A family of bush pigs rootle in a forest clearing, a shaggy sloth bear ambles through the forest, porcupines rustle their quills as they edge through the undergrowth, and a crocodile sunbathes on a sandbank. High up on the rocky crest, a spotted leopard sprawls along a branch eyeing up the local troop of langur monkeys. Its smaller relatives, the wild cats, prowl the

Left: silver langur
Top right –
clockwise: mango
fruit; banyan trees;
leopard; chittal

grass like household mogs on a spree. Jackals and hyenas circle restlessly looking for the leavings of someone else's meal. A python slithers off leaving behind a twisting trail. The *Jungle Book* is alive and well.

OFF-BEAT SAFARIS

Rural Rajasthan is at the heart of a tourist revolution as more and more opportunities arise to get out of the cities, into the villages, hills and deserts, to camp under the stars or stay in village forts, travelling by jeep, horse and camel. Prices and comfort levels vary enormously. Ask around, find out exactly what you are getting before you book, and don't allow yourselves to be swayed by high pressure sales techniques. Essential supplies include a hat, sun-block, water bottle, and lip salve, and for overnight trips, a long-sleeved shirt, mosquito repellent, torch and sleeping bag. It can get very cold at night in the desert.

CASTLE BIJAIPUR

This well-restored 16th-century fort next to a wildlife sanctuary in the Mewar hills acts as a centre for trekking, jeeps,

CAMELS

Camels are crucial to the economy of the desert, a source of food (both milk and meat), transport and clothing, and even a symbol of wealth. You can buy one whole and alive, or in a multitude of guises from *pattus*, huge camel wool shawls, and camel wool seats to camel hide jars and waterbottles, paintings, slippers or hats, and even toy camels made from camel skin. There are two distinct types in Rajasthan. Jaisalmer riding camels are smaller and swifter, standing about 2.2m high, weighing about 550kg. Bikaneri camels are the workhorses, 2.6m tall, weighing about 680kg. Both can travel 35 to 40km a day. Saddles, girths and bridles have almost inevitably become a local art form.

camping, boating, horse and camel safaris.

About 40km from Chittorgarh. Reservations from the Hotel Pratap Palace, Chittorgarh (tel: (01472) 2099).

BIKANER

Bikaner is way out in the desert, with dunes in easy reach. It is not yet as well known as Jaisalmer for its camel safaris, but there are still plenty on offer and, until other travellers catch up, you can get even further away from civilisation.

Camelmen

Opposite Sophia School, Jaipur Road (tel: 26416).

Rajasthan Safaris and Treks

Bassi House, Purani Ginani (tel: 28557).

Victor Travels and Tours

Behind Junargarh Fort, near Mahilamandal School (tel: 25626).

JAISALMER

Every second person in Jaisalmer offers camel safaris. What most people do is a gentle little trip to the Sam Dunes, about 40km from town. Here, literally hundreds of people are loaded, double-decker, on to camels and walked up the dunes, followed by little boys selling Limca. At the top, they dismount, watch the sunset, then solemnly ride down again. Hardier options include trips lasting several days, sleeping under the desert stars.

Sahara Travels

Jeep and camel safaris. The company is best known for its owner, 'Mr Desert', winner for several years of the Desert Festival men's beauty pageant, and now a familiar sight on advertising posters for the region.

First Fort Gate (tel: 2609).

A must for all travellers

JODHPUR

Several companies offer village safaris in the surrounding countryside. By far the most entertaining are those run by the Maharaja's eccentric uncle, Swaroop Singh, owner of the enchanting Ajit Bhawan Hotel. Small groups are taken out by jeep to a wide variety of villages. You get a real insight into the workings of rural Rajasthan but are also party to a fascinating vision of an upper-class Indian visiting 'his people'.

Ajit Bhawan Palace Hotel, near Circuit House, Airport Road (tel: 37410).

SHAHPURA PALACE

Camel and village safaris in the Shekhavati region of central Rajasthan, based on a restored 200-year-old palace, still run by the local ruling family.

65km from Jaipur on the Delhi Road. Details and booking: Shahpura House Guesthouse, D-257 Devi Marg, Bani Park, Jaipur 302 016 (tel: 77293).

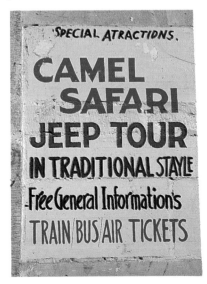

SHEKHAVATI

The little known area of Shekhavati, filling the gap between Bikaner, Jaipur and Alwar, was originally a province of Jaipur. It takes its name from Rao Shekhaji (1433–88) who declared independence in 1471. The kingdom never grew to rival its magnificent neighbours, has no major cities, and its numerous smaller forts and palaces are all small. It was home however to a remarkable band of Marwari merchants (see page 108) who followed the money when the trade routes shifted from the desert camel caravans to the sea. From the mid-18th to mid-20th centuries, they made vast fortunes which they spent on building grand *havelis* in their home towns and villages.

The typical three- to five-storey Rajasthani *haveli* (literally 'enclosed space') follows a pattern familiar from India's great Moghul palaces. Inward facing, it has blind walls and formidable gates to shut out the world, shaded colonnades to block the ferocious sun and a cool, breezy water-filled central courtyard as a place of relaxation. Many of the Shekhavati *havelis* are elaborately painted, if you are allowed inside – most are still private residences. You will also find wonderfully vivid frescoes in some of the temples and memorial *chhatris*. Fresco painting continued until about 1930, and the style evolved continuously with Muslim and Hindu traditional themes beside rampant animals and even colonial society ladies, cars and aeroplanes. The most interesting towns in the region include Jhunjhunu, Dundlod, Mandawa, Nawalgarh, Ramgarh, Bissau, and Fatehpur.

Tourist Information Office, Hotel Shiv Shekhewati, Khemi Sati Road, Jhunjhunu (tel: 2651 PP). Fatehpur, Nawalgarh and Jhunjhunu are on the railway, but the only really satisfactory way to tour is by car. Several local palaces are being turned into very comfortable, beautiful and often expensive small hotels, most of which offer village and desert tours, by jeep, camel or horse. Other accommodation options are scarce and spartan.

Brightly painted *havelis* are the hallmark of the Shekhavati region

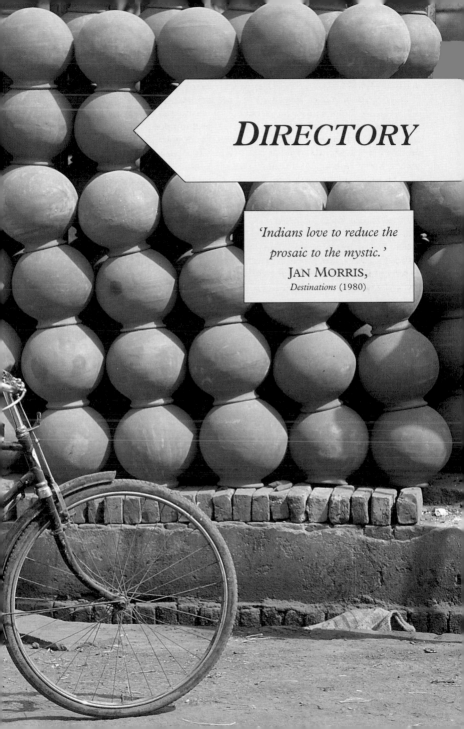

DIRECTORY

'Indians love to reduce the
prosaic to the mystic.'
JAN MORRIS,
Destinations (1980)

Shopping

At a time when many Indians' taste is veering towards nylon and plastic, the tourist trade has revived India's traditional craftsmanship. Rajasthan is a superb Aladdin's cave, rich with silk and silver and all the colours of the rainbow. Even if you normally hate shopping and despise souvenirs, now is the time to change your mind.

HOW TO SHOP

The constant hassle on the street is deeply irritating, but take your time and shop around. Have a drink, get a feel for your subject, gauge the price range and don't be swayed into parting with your money, however persistent or charming someone is, until you are ready. You are surrounded by some of the finest salesmen in the world and it is very hard to resist. Once you know what you want, start haggling. Don't believe anyone who says the post and packing will be free, don't get sucked into any dubious resale schemes, however plausible, and assume that all 'antiques' are fake. If genuine, they should have a certificate of authentication and you will need customs' clearance before you can export them. If you are buying something expensive and having it posted, pay by credit card so you are insured if it doesn't turn up.

WHAT TO BUY

Carpets

A close second to those of Iran or Kashmir, luxuriant, close-knotted silk and wool pile carpets are best found in Jaipur and Delhi. Bikaner specialises in cheap and cheerful *namdahs*, embroidered on felt, and brightly coloured cotton-weave *durries* are widely made in eastern Rajasthan and around Agra.

Jewellery

There is costume jewellery aplenty, from bright bangles and beads of lac (enamel) and glass to gorgeous, heavy tribal designs in silver and semi-precious stones. There is also a thriving market in loose gems, and superbly crafted jewellery in both Western and Indian designs. Prices for genuine articles are very reasonable, but it is a minefield of fraud. Unless you know what you are doing, or know someone who does, be very, very careful. See also pages 154–5.

A few of India's many local crafts

Puppets have a distinguished history here – and are also great gifts

Miniature paintings

The crudest are mass-produced paintings by numbers, but you can buy pleasing creations on either paper or silk at a very affordable price. Use a magnifying glass to look at the detail of the brushstrokes. A speciality of Udaipur, they are available everywhere. See pages 130–1.

Pottery

The best pottery around is charming Jaipur blue ware, made from fuller's earth, quartz and sodium sulphite. Traditional designs use only blues, turquoise and white, but some greens, yellows and browns are now creeping in.

Stonework

Agra has a thriving tradition of *pietra dura* – beautifully crafted, delicate inlay of semi-precious stones on marble. Numerous factory shops sell plates, trays and even tables, as well as cheaper work on soapstone. At Fatehpur Sikri, some

1,500 people make their living carving 'pregnant' elephants, frogs, and other animals of soapstone.

Textiles

Go to Jaipur for tie-dye, block prints and delicate fabrics such as silk saris; Jaisalmer for rich mirrored embroidery, patchworks and appliqué; and to Bikaner for heavy, coarse weaves of rough wool. Also look for superb Kashmir wool jackets, shawls and stoles at very reasonable prices. See also pages 154–5.

Other buys

Puppets and other **toys** (mostly poor quality and unsuitable for small children); **leatherwork**, from camel skin bags to embroidered slippers; **embossed** and/or **enamelled brassware** (the finest work is based on silver and even gold); **essential oils**, made up to your own recipe; **spices**; **books** (on India, but also cheap English-language editions)... the list is endless.

WHERE TO SHOP

The easiest way to shop is to head for a state-run emporium or hotel shopping mall, where you should be reasonably certain that prices are fair and your silk is not polyester or your carpet nylon. However, do be very careful because most shops calling themselves government emporia and other official-sounding names are actually privately owned and will try anything they think they can get away with. The Rajasthali chain is managed by the Rajasthan Tourism Development Corporation and every state in India has an official outlet in Delhi. Delhi, Jaipur and, to a lesser extent, Jaisalmer are the oustandingly good shopping centres.

More fun are the factory shops where you can see anything from painting to inlay work, weaving to enamel in production. These are worth a visit even if you are not looking to buy. Remember that anywhere you are taken by a driver or guide will involve a commission – anything from 5 per cent to 20 per cent. On the other hand, some of them know some very good places that you could never find on your own. By all means go with them. After all, you are allowed to say no.

Finally, India has markets in abundance, with open-air market stalls, selling fruit and vegetables, spices and dyes, mind and nose numbing meat markets filled with flies and scrawny dogs. Around every temple is a cluster of stalls selling coconuts and marigolds, strings of jasmine and fire crackers as offerings to the gods. You need a zip replaced or a shoe mended? Turn your head and someone will be waiting, cross-legged under a tree, needle in hand. A grotesque set of battered plastic teeth marks the pitch of the pavement dentist.

Best of all are the bazaars, their endless narrow streets and alleys of tiny, dark cubby-hole shops filled with the glitter of gold, the slither of crimson silk, and the sizzle of boiling oil. The air is pungent with attar of roses, cardamom, garlic, stale urine and incense. Eager shop keepers hurl bolt after bolt of fabric, carpet after carpet, sailing through the air in a glorious rainbow of colour and texture. Strings of beads cluster plumply in the doorways, great stacks of globular cooking pots gleam dimly from the shadows, sculptures of marble and soapstone, sandalwood and bronze squat on heavily laden shelves. From every doorway comes the cry, 'You want...? Just look..?' – it's hard to resist.

DELHI

The Bookworm

Probably the best of Delhi's bookshops with a wide range of books on India as well as general titles.
B-29 Connaught Place. Tel: 332 2260.

Narayan Jewellers

Fine array of modern and traditional jewellery.
Ground Floor, 27 Barakhamba Road. Tel: 331 152/3.

Multi-Craft Emporia
Central Cottage Industries Emporium

The excellent government-run outlet for the entire country.
Janpath. Tel: 332 8506.

Cottage Industries Exposition Ltd

DCM Building, 16 Barakhamba Road. Tel: 331 4479/331 3833.

Handicrafts and Handloom Export Corp Showroom

Lok Kalyan Bhawan, 11A Rouse Avenue Lane. Tel: 331 1086.

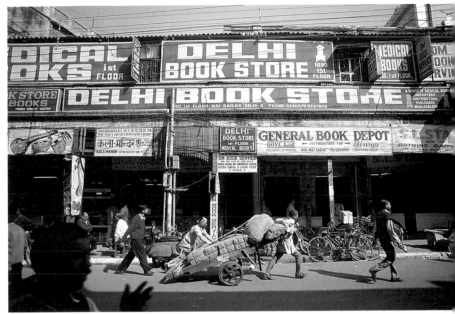

Search carefully and you'll find everything in Delhi, but shops look very different

Trans Asian Industries Exposition Ltd

M-1, Hauz Khas, Main Mehrauli Road, New Delhi 110 016. Tel: 668 685/686 5692.

Good Shopping Areas

Baba Kharak Singh Marg
All the different states of India have showcase State Emporia strung along this road near Connaught Place and Janpath.

Connaught Place
The whole area is filled by street stalls as well as proper shops.

Hauz Khas Village
Up-market selection of designer boutiques in restored village houses.
Near Deer Park, South Extension.

Santushti Shopping Arcade
Excellent shopping arcade with numerous good shops including Anokhi (tel: 688 3076). See Jaipur.
Opposite Samrat Hotel, Chanakyapuri.

Best Markets
Janpath – good cheap souvenirs in the Tibetan Market.
Chandni Chowk – Old Delhi's main shopping area for the last 350 years. Good for perfume, jewellery and carpets. See also page 48.
Karol Bagh – along Panchkuin Marg, north of Connaught Place. Traditionally the furniture market.

A whole raft of daily markets shifts around the city. The best example is probably the Friday Market, which takes place beside the Red Fort.

AGRA

Agra tends to be very expensive. Shop in Delhi or Jaipur for preference.

Oswal Emporium
30 Munro Road, Agra Cantt. Tel: 75168.

UP Handicraft Palace
49 Bansal Nagar. Tel: 68214.
Both these shops have a wide range of products including *pietra dura* inlay.
The best shopping areas are beside the Taj entrance, Mahatma Gandhi Road and Gwalior Road. Markets include Sadar Bazaar, Kinari Bazaar, and Pratap Pura.

Old and new antiques for sale

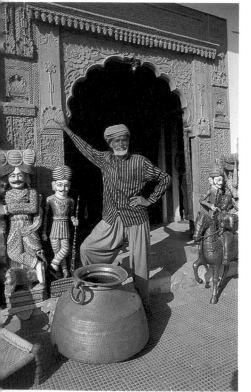

BIKANER

Abhivyakti
Outlet for the charitable Urmul Trust. Beautiful heavy ethnic weave fabrics, shawls, cushion covers etc.
Inside Junagarh Fort.

JAIPUR

Anokhi
Wonderful hand printed clothes, soft furnishings and accessories. Home base of an international designer chain, with much lower prices than outlets abroad..
2 Yudhistra Marg behind Secretariat. Tel: 381 619.

Bhurumal Rajmal Surana
For the rich. Superbly made traditional Indian jewellery, dripping with gems.
Lal Katra, Johari Bazar. Tel: 560 628/561 440.

Khadi Ghar
Handloomed Indian cotton.
MI Road. Tel: 73745.

Omdain
Finely crafted traditional gold and silver jewellery.
228–9 Johari Bazaar, Jaipur 302 003. Tel: 560 489.

Rajasthali
Government emporium, with wide range of fixed price souvenirs.
Ajmeri Gate, MI Road. Tel: 367 176.

Rajputana Carpets
One of several fine carpet factories in the area, with guided tours and a showroom stuffed with treasures.
Near Dashera Kothi, Govind Nagar (East), Amber Road. Tel: 45635; 42870.

Markets
The whole of the old city is effectively one massive market. Try Ramganj Bazaar for handmade and embroidered leather footwear; Badi Chaupar, Johari Bazaar or Jadiyon-ka-Rasta, Gopalji-ka-

Rasta, and Haldiyon-ka-Rasta, for jewellery; Maniharon-ka-Rasta, off Tripolia Bazaar, for lac bangles; Khajanewalon-ka-Rasta, off Chandpol Bazaar, for stone carving; Hawa Mahal area for antiques, fake antiques, quilts; and Johari Bazaar for textiles. For the finest block prints and handmade marbled paper, head 8km out of town to the suburb of Sanganer.

JAISALMER
Central Jaisalmer is one huge souvenir shop. Particularly strong areas are by the Fort Gate, around the Jain Temples, and near the *havelis*. The shops inside the *havelis* are good, but comparatively expensive.
Rajasthali and **Khadi Bandar** are both just outside Amar Sagar Gate.

JODHPUR
Abbani Handicraft
High Court Road, near Tourist Bungalow. Tel: 44550.
Lucky Silk Palace
Sojari Gate. Tel: 2222/2422.
Mohanlal Verhomal
Wonderful spice shop, selling also outside the Fort Gate and mail order.
Shop No. 209B, Vegetable Market, Clock Tower (no telephone).
Rajasthan Art Emporium
One of a long strip of enticing antique shops.
Umaid Bhawan Palace Road. Tel: 36761.

Emporia cluster around Sojari Gate, and factory shops gather around Siwanchai and Jalori Gates. Markets include Sardar Market, Clock Tower, Station Road (for jewellery), Tripolia Bazaar (for crafts), Khanda Falsa (for tie-dye), Lakhara Bazaar (for lac), Mochi Bazaar (for shoes).

Elaborate textiles and embroidery are a local speciality, cheap and portable

UDAIPUR
Jagdish Emporium
Wide range of handicrafts including fine textiles.
City Palace Road.
Rajasthali
Fixed price government emporium.
Chetak Circle. Tel: 28768.
Good souvenir shopping areas include Chetak Circle, Hathipole (the outer court of the City Palace), Palace Road and Shastri Circle. Markets include Bapu Bazaar, Clock Tower, Nehru Bazaar, Sindhi Bazaar, Bada Bazaar.

A SYMPHONY OF COLOUR

Against a background of dusty land and sun-bleached skies, Rajasthan is filled with opulent colour, the sparkle of mirror and silver and precious stones, the shimmer of silk, and vivid kaleidoscope of cotton.

Tribal jewellery is mainly silver, copper and bronze, bold, beautiful and huge. Women literally wear the family silver in a jangle of necklaces and clatter of bangles, with ivory or bone bracelets on the upper arm to show their married status. There are two traditions of classical jewellery. Jazzy *kundan* work is the art of setting small stones, jewels or crystals, in a complex pattern of 24-carat gold. *Meenakari* is the art of enamelling, etched into a base metal, or in the case of jewellery, gold. The finest pieces combine both, the front bright with shining stones, the back a perfectly crafted enamel mosaic.

Perhaps even more fabulous are the fabrics. The men are usually responsible for weaving, dyeing and tailoring the cloth, and for the sumptuous gold *zardosi* embroidery used on festive saris. The women handle the delicate tying of knots for gaudy *bandhari* work, infinitely intricate tie-dye, with pin-head wisps of material tightly bound and rebound to create

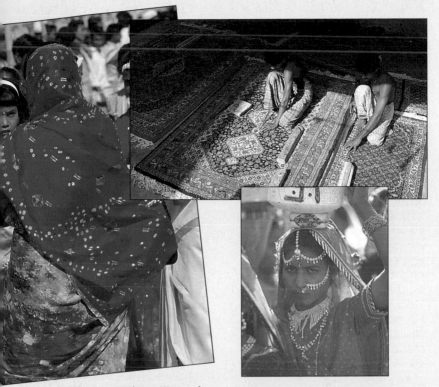

complex patterns of dots, circles, squares and stripes, and the elaborate embroidery and appliqué which covers their bodices and waistcoats with heavy patterns and shining mirror fragments. Traditional dyes included iron and indigo, jasmine, pistachio, saffron and mulberry; these days they are usually chemical. Shot cottons are woven with a warp and weft of different colours while the Alwar area specialises in dyeing the front and back of the cloth in different hues and Sanganer, just outside Jaipur, is renowned for its block prints, hand stamped designs, using carved wooden

Tie-dye, appliqué and embroidery, cotton and silk, heavy silver rings and fragile gold filigree – local crafts are thriving and exquisite

blocks as templates.

The materials are familiar in Europe. Eighteenth-century noblemen's *bandhari* handkerchiefs gave their name to the bandana, while the women decked themselves out in sprigged muslin, finest block print cottons. Today, Rajasthani textiles and jewellery are beginning to creep back on to the designers' catwalks at the forefront of the '90s ethnic revolution.

Entertainment

DELHI

Delhi has all the entertainment you could hope for in a major international city. What is not produced locally comes with international tours of everything from symphonies to rock. Theatre is usually in Hindi, although there are some touring productions and amateur groups do work in English. France, Italy, Britain, Germany and the USA all have cultural institutes with touring lectures and regular films. Some of the international hotels have discos or cabarets, at a price, and there are several good venues for cultural programmes of Indian music and dance. As everywhere in India, there are numerous cinemas showing first run mainstream films in English as well as a huge array of Hindi 'Bollywood' blockbusters. A useful weekly booklet, *Delhi Diary*, has full entertainment listings and lots of other up-to-date tourist and practical information. It should be available at all hotels.

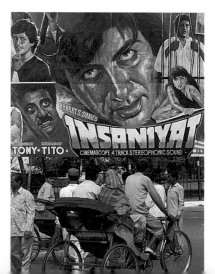

AUDITORIA AND GALLERIES

These are all multi-purpose cultural venues which house a range of exhibitions, lectures, dance, theatre and music.

ICCR
Azad Bhawan, Indraprashtra Estate (tel: 331 2274).

Kamani Auditorium
Copernicus Marg (tel: 388 084).

Triveni Kala Sangam
205 Tansen Marg (tel: 371 8833).

CULTURAL PROGRAMMES

The Village Bistro
Excellent entertainment programme featuring tribal and classical dance and music from right across India, set in the Hauz Khas ruins. See also page 51.
12 Hauz Khas Village, near Deer Park (tel: 685 3857, 665 445, 685 2226 or 685 2227). Nightly at 6.45pm and 7.45pm.

Dances of India
Programme of classic, folk and tribal dances.
Anjuman Hall, Bahadur Shah Zafar Marg, near Delhi Gate (tel: 331 7831/332 0968). Nightly at 6.45pm.

Son-et-Lumière
Nightly tour of Moghul history, set in the Red Fort grounds.
Red Fort (tel: 600 121 extn 2156/274 4580 after 5pm). Hindi and English: times vary according to season, so check locally). Admission charge.

DISCOS

Oasis
Hyatt Regency, Bhikaji Cama Place, Ring Road (tel: 609 911).

India makes more films than Hollywood

Drums play an important role in tribal music

Ghungroo
Maurya Sheraton, Diplomatic Enclave,
Chanakyapuri (tel: 301 0101).
No 1
Taj Mahal, Mansingh Road (tel: 301
6162).

ELSEWHERE

Once outside Delhi, the options drop off
dramatically, although you will still find
at least one cultural programme and
several cinemas in any large town. The
best way to occupy yourself in the early
evenings is to head for the markets which
buzz with excitement. It is also where you
will find any street entertainers.

AGRA
Taj Khema
Nightly folk dance and music programme
in restaurant garden, with views of the
Taj Mahal.
Eastern Gate, Taj Road (no telephone).

JAIPUR
Rajputana Palace Sheraton
Nightly performance of music, dance and
puppetry in an open-air theatre in the
hotel gardens, 7pm–9pm.
Palace Road. Tel: 62031/68254.

JODHPUR
Ghoomar Tourist Bungalow
High Court Road. Tel: 21900.
Sangeet Natak Academy
Folk dancing in high season only. Details
from the Tourist Office (tel: 45083).
Paota 'B' Road.
Also displays at the Ajit Bhawan and
Umaid Bhawan Hotels (see pages 168–9).

UDAIPUR
Bhartiya Lok Kala Mandal
Some of the finest displays in Rajasthan,
with an internationally acclaimed puppet
troop and regional dance and music.
Near Chetak Circle. Tel: 29296. Daily,
6–7pm. Admission charge.
Lake Palace Hotel
Puppet shows at 7pm, dance at 9pm
daily for guests and diners only.
Lake Pichola. Tel: 23241.
Meera Kala Mandir
Nightly dance and music performances.
City Station Road. Tel: 83176. Daily,
7–8pm. Admission charge.

Festivals

*T*he Hindu calendar is a continuous stream of festivities in celebration of every major and minor god, the seasons, and rites of passage. Most are basically private and never touch the visitor, but plenty are spectacular, filled with music and dance, fire crackers and processions. Added to these are the huge fairs or *melas*, cattle or camel markets. Most major festivals celebrate more than one god or event and stretch over several days.

REPUBLIC DAY

India's most spectacular parade is along the Rajpath in New Delhi.
Representative 'floats' from all over India include highly ornamented elephants, camels, horses, dancers and musicians, and a military procession. Tickets for seats are sold months ahead (contact Thomas Cook, page 188).

DESERT FESTIVAL

Totally for tourists, the Jaisalmer Desert Festival is noisy and colourful, with camel races, a Mr Desert 'beauty' pageant, best moustache competition etc. There is also a Desert Festival in Bikaner.

HOLI

The traditional Hindu festival of colour celebrates the end of winter, the destruction of the demon Holika, Kama, god of love, and his wife, Rati, goddess of passion. People mark the day by bombarding each other with coloured water, dye or, in poorer villages, watery

---

JANUARY/FEBRUARY
Nagaur Fair (Ramdeoji Cattle Fair) – Nagaur
Desert Festival – Jaisalmer
Republic Day (26th Jan) – Delhi
Beating the Retreat (29th Jan) – Delhi
Baneshwar – tribal festival of the Bheel people
Sakrant – Delhi

FEBRUARY/MARCH
Holi – everywhere.
Elephant Festival – Jaipur (during Holi)

MARCH/APRIL
Gangaur – across Rajasthan. The Mewar Festival in Udaipur coincides.

JUNE
Summer Festival – Mount Abu

JULY/AUGUST
Teej – everywhere; best seen in Jaipur.
Kalji Teej – Bundi

SEPTEMBER/OCTOBER
Marwar Festival – Jodhpur
Dussehra – everywhere; processions in Jaipur and a Mela (fair) in Kota.

OCTOBER/NOVEMBER
Pushkar Mela – Pushkar
Kolagat Mela – Bikaner
Chandrabhaga Kartik Fair – Jhalrapatan, near Jhalawar.
Diwali – everywhere.

clay and cattle dung, and by drinking marijuana-based *bhang*. In Jaipur, there is a splendid accompanying Elephant Festival.

GANGAUR
Primarily a women's festival, celebrating married bliss and fertility. Images of Gan and Gauri (Shiva and Parvati) are decorated and carried in procession, with dancing and music.

TEEJ
Celebrating the reunion of Shiva and Parvati and the onset of the monsoon, women dress up in their best and take turns on the brightly decorated swings. There are processions, with idols, elephants, traditional songs and dance.

DUSSEHRA
A popular 10-day festival, celebrating the victories of the goddess Durga over the demon, Mahishasaura, and Rama over the demon king, Ravana. People perform the Ram Lila (story of the *Ramayana*) and burn effigies of the demons. The 10th day, traditionally the start of the military campaigning season, is marked by a magnificent procession in Jaipur.

DIWALI
The Festival of Lights is the biggest event of the Hindu calendar, marking the New Year. Everything, everywhere is lit up by candles, oil lamps and even fairy lights, to light Rama's path on his journey home. The accompanying fire crackers sound like the Blitz. People traditionally give each other sweets, and spring clean their houses in honour of the fastidious goddess, Lakshmi.

PUSHKAR MELA
Over the full moon of Kartik Poornima,

up to 200,000 Hindu pilgrims come to bathe in the sacred lake. Alongside them is one of India's largest cattle, camel and horse fairs. Finally, Pushkar now attracts some 50,000 foreign tourists a year, and huge tented villages and entertainment programmes are laid on to keep them amused.

The Rajasthan Tourism Development Corporation sets up tented villages at the most entertaining festival sites. Book through any RTDC office.

Festivals are all peacock-displays of vibrant colour

Children

*A*lthough India has more children of its own than almost any other country in the world, this is not the ideal destination, especially for babies and small children, with very real health hazards (see pages 182–3). Once into their teens, however, they should have built up enough stamina and natural immunity and the situation is very different.

BASIC SURVIVAL

Try and base yourself in one place, preferably in a good hotel with a swimming pool. The chef will normally be happy to make up fresh food to your instructions, with some warning, but take an emergency supply of bottled baby food in case. Chips and biscuits, hard boiled eggs, bananas and bottled fizz are available everywhere and make up an adequate survival diet for slightly older children, if the worst comes to the worst. The hotel should be able to organise a competent baby sitter for you. It is not really a good idea to hire your own nanny as most are uneducated women with very different standards of hygiene and safety to your own. Take a full supply of disposable nappies (the local version leaks and chaps). Do your sightseeing in relatively small chunks and read up ahead of time, the area is filled with wonderful legends and stories, sufficient to keep any self-respecting child enthralled. Some sort of diary and/or collection will help focus their attention.

The biggest problems spring from kindness. Indians adore Western children. Your child will act as a magnet, with people crowding in close to see and touch. Never mind the cleanliness of the hands, most children hate being pawed or crowded. Kind Indian mothers will also feed your child unhygienic drinks or snacks, so you must be both vigilant and diplomatic. Finally, India is full of potential wonders for children, from fairground rides held together with an elastic band to streetsellers laden with badly made and poisonous toys. Even the balloons may have been blown up by a TB sufferer.

THINGS TO DO

Transport
Just getting around can be an adventure. Auto- and cycle rickshaws will be great favourites, and trains will also be

Indian children love to talk to tourists

popular, especially if you can find a last, lurking steam engine. In Jaipur, take them to Amber for an elephant ride.

In Town

The forts are sufficiently dramatic to avoid becoming boring old museums, especially if you can find good details like the staggered gates, designed to stop a charging elephant or an infant Maharajah's cradles and toys. Some temples, like the Karna Mati temple near Bikaner with its sacred rats, provide better entertainment than others, but nobody seems to mind too much if your children play aeroplanes around the courtyard. The markets are lively and colourful and noisy and there is plenty of street entertainment with musicians and snake charmers and puppets. Where there are lakes, there are usually pedaloes and rowing boats and every town has at least one good park with space for running and shade for exhausted parents.

Out of Town

Older children will probably enjoy a desert safari, whether by jeep, camel or horse, at least as much as you. Ranthambore and Sariska offer tiger hunting (with a camera) while Bharatpur is not only fascinating for its birds, but allows you to walk in the bush and look for pythons.

Delhi

Delhi has several specially designed attractions.

The Bal Bhavan and National Children Museum

1 Kotla Road, New Delhi (tel: 331 4701). Open: Tuesday to Saturday, 9am–5.30pm; miniature trains run 12.30–5.30pm.

Shankar's International Dolls Museum (see page 43)

The **Zoo** and the **Appu Ghar** fairground are both on Pragati Maidan.

Cricket is a national obsession

Sport

*A*lthough few foreigners think of India as a sporting destination (with the exception perhaps of the mountain sports in the Himalayas), it does have almost everything on offer, mainly for the local middle and upper classes. Rajasthan, however, is not one of the best equipped regions in the country. The traditional sports of the Maharajas were hunting (now banned), military skills such as sword play (now, hopefully, not needed) and expensive pastimes like polo, still played but only by the rich. The poor have always worked too hard to want much more exercise and the heat is enough to dissuade most people. Cricket, not football, is the national obsession. India also excels internationally in hockey and table tennis.

ADVENTURE SPORTS

At present, there are few adventure sports available in this region, other than a little gentle rock climbing near Delhi. Rajasthan is beginning to build up a programme however, concentrating first on providing watersports such as windsurfing, sailing and waterskiing on some of the larger lakes.

CRICKET

Cricket is the favoured game of little boys from villages to dusty city backstreets and their fathers, who eagerly spend their hard-earned rupees to crowd into noisy matches. Great cricketers are heroes, as big as pop and movie stars and test cricket has the stature of the FA cup or Rosebowl.

GOLF

Golf is beginning to catch on amongst middle class businessmen, thanks to visiting expats (the Japanese in particular). Delhi has two fine courses and there are also courses in each of the main cities. Most are open to visitors.

HEALTH AND FITNESS

Many of the 5-star de luxe hotels have some sort of Western-style gymnasium, sauna and jacuzzi tucked away somewhere within their walls, but health and fitness activities Indian-style are far more likely to involve Ayurvedic massage, herbal steam baths, yoga and meditation.

POLO

The polo season is nowhere near as frenetic as it was 50 years ago, but Delhi, Jaipur and Jodhpur all still have grounds on the international circuit. Locals also play the game on camels, bicycles and even elephants. The polo-playing season lasts from November until March. Check local listings or with the tourist office for matches.

SWIMMING

There are very few public pools around and swimming in the disease-laden natural water is not really a good idea. Most 5-star hotels and the sporting clubs have good pools however, and many are prepared to open them up to non-residents, for the payment of a fee (usually about Rs100). The list of amenable hotels tends to change frequently, but there will usually be at least one available to the public in every large town or city.

India's test cricketers are national heroes

DELHI CLUBS

Delhi Golf Club

18 holes, 220 acres, 200 species of trees and shrubs, 300 species of birds and numerous Lodi tombs and monuments. Casual membership and equipment hire available.

Dr Zakir Hussein Marg (tel: 699 236).

Delhi Polo Club

Casual membership, tickets for tournaments and information on polo throughout India.

President's Estate, Rashtrapati Bhawan (tel: 375 604).

The Meadows Golf and Country Club

Delightful 18-hole golf course and open air restaurant, bar, health club and pool. Cottage accommodation. Low green fees and equipment to hire.

F-4/7 Vasant Vihar, New Delhi (tel: 687 2274); on the Gurgaon–Sohna Road, 4km from the Gurgaon Roundabout.

The Resort Country Club

Luxurious country club with golf, tennis, bowling, target shooting and swimming; mini-golf, badminton, croquet, billiards and table tennis. Also children's entertainment such as pony and camel rides. Also a bar, restaurant and cottage-style accommodation.

Pachgaon–Mohamedpur Road, V&PO Hasanpur (Dist Gurgaon), Harayana (tel: 122 105). About 30km from Delhi, off the Jaipur Road.

Delhi has several major sporting stadiums hosting a range of home-grown and international events. Check local listings (*Delhi Diary* and the newspapers) to see what is on where.

Food and Drink

*W*estern foodies tend by nature to scorn the hotel dining rooms and try to hunt out the little backstreet bistro that no one else has discovered. In India, this can be a bad mistake. There are a few exceptions, but most of the really good restaurants are run by the hotels – and the Indians know it too. Here you will find not only the cream of cuisines, from Mughlai to South Indian, French, or Thai, but lavish (and incredibly reasonable) lunchtime buffets, and 24-hour coffee shops for the chilli-weary palate. Only rarely will you find yourself in a tourist ghetto.

FORMICA AND FLIES

Once out of this rarified atmosphere, the average Indian restaurant has strip lighting, sticky formica table tops, a

menu running to several pages with Indian and Chinese (second favourite) and Continental food. Indian cuisine can be some of the finest in the world (see pages 170–1). Sadly, however, the good stuff is all cooked at home, behind closed doors and what you are usually offered is dire. The menu lists hundreds of mouth-watering possibilities, all so heavily spiced and oily they taste the same, and everything but the mutton stew is probably off. The good news is that there are always plenty of vegetarian options. Meat is almost always chicken or mutton (goat). It is forbidden for Hindus to eat beef (any steak will be buffalo) and pork is anathema to Muslims. Fish is best avoided in these inland areas.

Continental food is a horrifying mix of multi-national institutional and England *c* 1930s. Breakfast includes cornflakes or lumpy porridge with boiling milk, grey spongy omelettes, and elastic off-white toast with virulently coloured and totally tasteless jam. For lunch and dinner, you can have overcooked spaghetti with something nasty, red and nameless smeared across it, more omelettes and cold soggy chips (known as finger chips to avoid confusion with crisps, which are also chips).

Bubbling cauldrons of Indian fast food

Fizzy drinks are less enticing but much safer than fresh fruit juice

STREET EATING

Normal travelling wisdom says to avoid street stalls. However some of India's most popular restaurants are streetside *dhabas*, with long trestle tables and bubbling cauldrons. They normally keep things simple, serving a basic *thali* to everyone. The turnover is huge, so the food is always fresh and you can watch it cooking to allay any lingering doubts. Indians prefer using their fingers to forks (right hand only, using the left is a grave social blunder).

No matter where you eat, hygiene must be the first consideration (see Health, page 182). If you are not used to eating spicy foods regularly, don't expect to be able to survive a solid diet of chillies without trouble. There are non-hot options if you look, while simple foods such as plain rice, chapatis and yoghurt are excellent if you feel ill. Take a few muesli bars or biscuits as iron rations.

DRINKS

Fizzy drinks, cartons of fruit juice and bottled mineral water are freely available. Familiar names include Coke, Pepsi and Sprite. Local versions include Thums Up (cola), Gold Spot (orange) and Limca (lemon). A refreshing alternative is fresh lime soda. Yoghurt-based *lassis* come sweet, plain or salted, and also help mop up the hottest spices. Weak instant coffee is usually available, but tea (*chai*) is more usual in north India. It normally comes with the milk and huge quantities of sugar all boiled in together. Specify when ordering that you want separate or 'tray' tea, without sugar. Alcohol is virtually unobtainable outside the tourist hotels and is never served in ordinary restaurants. The most common local beer, Kingfisher, is very palatable. The local versions of most spirits are fine if drowned. The imported variety and wine are astronomically expensive.

WHERE TO EAT

Prices

The following categories are based on the cost of a full meal for one, without alcohol. It is possible to eat much more cheaply, for only a few rupees if you go to the street stalls and small cafés.

R – 75–150 rupees
RR– 150–350 rupees
RRR – above 350 rupees

DELHI

Broadway Hotel RR

Indian and Continental food and snazzy décor (a salad bar in a vintage car). Near the Red Fort and popular after the *son-et-lumière*. Booking advised.
4/15 Asafali Road (tel: 327 3821).

Dasaprakash RR

Excellent and very friendly South Indian restaurant. Happy to give you a whistle-stop guide to the cuisine and to tone down the sometimes rather ferocious spices.
Hotel Ambassador, Sujan Singh Park (tel: 463 2600).

Kabila RR

Comfortable restaurant serving good Mughlai food and, unusually, with a bar.
1st Floor, DDA Local Shopping Centre, Aurobindo Place, Hauz Khas (tel: 668 494/686 4920).

Maurya Sheraton RRR

A de luxe hotel with several acclaimed restaurants, including the **Bukhara** tandoor, classed amongst the great restaurants of the world, and the **Dum Phukt**, specialising in Mughlai cuisine.
Sardel Patel Marg, Diplomatic Enclave (tel: 301 0101).

Nirula's R

Slightly tatty but a travellers' institution, with good pizzas, burgers, pastries and ice-creams downstairs and Indian, Chinese and Continental restaurants upstairs.
L Block, Connaught Place (tel: 332 2419).

The Village Bistro RR–RRR

Out of the way in South Delhi, but worth the effort. A huge complex of eight restaurants, including Continental, South Indian vegetarian, North Indian, Chinese, kebab and tandoori cuisines and a rooftop barbecue overlooking the Hauz Khas ruins. The food is excellent; there is a cultural programme every evening (see page 156), live entertainment and souvenir shopping on tap.
12 Hauz Khas Village, near Deer Park, New Delhi (tel: 685 3857/665 445/685 2226/685 2227).

Other de luxe hotels with particularly good food include the Oberoi, Ashok, Taj Palace and Taj Mahal, all of which have several restaurants.

AGRA

Garden View Restaurant R

Indian, Italian, Mexican and Continental food.
Hotel Sakura, 48 Old Idgah Colony, near Idgah Bus Stand (no telephone).

Nauratna RRR

Excellent Mughlai restaurant in modern palace-style hotel.
Mughal Sheraton, Fatehabad Road, Taj Ganj (tel: 64701).

Novotel Brasserie RR

Indian and Continental food delivered with all the flair of this French-based

chain. The result is light, imaginative and mouthwatering.
Tajnagri Scheme, Fatehabad Road (tel: 368 282).

Only Restaurant R
Pleasant garden restaurant run by former Sheraton staff.
45 Taj Road, Crossing Fool Sayed (no telephone).

Taj Khema RR
The normal range of food, with a garden, good views of the Taj Mahal and folk dance and cultural programmes.
Eastern Gate, Taj Road (no telephone).

AJMER

Honey Dew Restaurant R
Cheap and reasonably cheerful, with Indian and Continental food.
Station Road, opposite the station (no telephone).

Hotel Mansingh Palace RR
Comfortable hotel with good coffee shop and dining room.
Vaishali Nagar, overlooking the lake (tel: 30855).

ALWAR

Hotel Sariska Palace RR
Converted former palace/hunting lodge.
Opp. Sariska Park entrance, 11km from Alwar (tel: 222).

BHARATPUR

Forest Lodge
Pleasant ITDC-run hotel and simple restaurant, best in Bharatpur.
Inside the bird sanctuary (tel: 2260/2322).

BIKANER

Amber R
Indian vegetarian food.
Station Road (tel: 61861).

Chotoo Matoo Restaurant R
Indian vegetarian food.
Station Road (tel: 24466).

Thar Hotel Restaurant R
Vegetarian and non-vegetarian Indian food, considered to be the best in town.
Near Ambadkhar Circle (tel: 27180).

Lalgarh Palace Restaurant RRR
Bikaner's only 5-star de luxe hotel in a former palace (see page 76) with a suitably grand restaurant and live entertainment.
Palace Road, about 4km north of town centre (tel: 61963).

Drinks on the lawn,
Jai Mahal Hotel, Jaipur

CHITTORGARH

Morcha Restaurant R
Pleasant and ordinary, the best option in town.
Hotel Pratap Palace, opp HPO (tel: 2099).

KOTA

Brijraj Bhawan Palace RR
A wonderful old royal palace, this is Kota's best hotel and restaurant by a long way.
Civil Lines (tel: 25203).

Palace View Garden Restaurant R
Open air vegetarian restaurant with North and South Indian, Chinese and Continental food.
Near Palace, Barrage Rd (no telephone).

JAIPUR

Chandralok RR
Traditional Rajasthani food in comfortable surroundings.
MI Road, above Laxshmi Commercial Bank.

LMB (Laxshmi Mishthan Bhandar) R
The travellers' stop right in the centre of the old town with good, cheap vegetarian food, both Indian and Western. Ice-.cream parlour in front, restaurant behind.
Johari Bazaar (tel: 565 844).

Niro's RR
Widely regarded as the best non-hotel restaurant in Jaipur and popular with locals. Normal huge menu with selections of Indian, Continental and Chinese food.
MI Road (tel: 374 493/383 187).

Rambagh Palace RRR
Built by Ram Singh II, this superb palace, home of later Maharajahs, was the only private residence in the world with its own polo ground. It is now Jaipur's grandest hotel. Come here for a drink at least, to wallow in the marble courts and peacock-festooned lawns. The food is excellent and the service impeccable. Several options include a formal dining room, a verandah barbecue and coffee shop.
Bhavani Singh Road (tel: 381241).

Other hotels with good dining rooms include the Jai Mahal, Rajputana Palace Sheraton, Hotel Man Singh, and Clarks Ajmer (all RRR) and the Gangaur Tourist Bungalow (R).

JAISALMER

Golden Fort R
Cheap and cheerful Indian and Continental food and a roof terrace with fort view and live music.
Hanuman Chouraha, off Collector's Office Road, near the Tourist Bungalow (tel: 2545).

Hotel Dhola Maru R
Modern hotel with bizarre basement dining room. The food is wonderful. Phone ahead to place your order.
Jethwai Road, 4km out of town (tel: 2761).

Trio R
Light, bright and popular, cheap rooftop terrace, with good Indian and Continental food.
Above Bank of Baroda, Gandhi Chowk, near Amar Sagar Gate (tel: 2733).

JODHPUR

Ajit Bhawan Palace Hotel RR
One-sitting dinner at 7.30pm each

evening in the palace courtyard, with dancers and musicians as well as good food and company. Book ahead.
Near Circuit House, Airport Rd (tel: 37410).

Gypsy/Frigo R

Two popular, cheap and cheerful fast food joints.
Sardarpura (tel: Gypsy – 33288 ; Frigo – 33212).

Kalinga R–RR

Popular travellers' hangout with good Mughlai, Rajasthani and Continental food.
Hotel Adarsh Niwas, Railway Station Road, directly opposite the station (tel: 27313/ 23658).

Pankaj R

Good Indian vegetarian food.
Jalori Gate (tel: 35540).

Umaid Bhawan Hotel RRR

The last palace ever built in Rajasthan; now Jodhpur's top hotel with a formal restaurant with an excellent lunchtime buffet, and a coffee shop. See also page 112.
Umaid Bhavan Road (tel: 22316).

MOUNT ABU

Hotel Hilltone

Modern and not as pretty as some of the palace hotels, but the food is better.
Central, just off the main road into town tel: 3112).

RANTHAMBORE

Sawai Madhopur Lodge

Former royal hunting lodge with an attractive garden, bar and restaurant.
About 5km from Sawai Madhopur, on the Ranthambore road (tel: 2541).

The delights of an outdoor feast, Ajit Bhawan, Jodhpur

UDAIPUR

Berry's Restaurant R

Simple, popular restaurant with Indian, Chinese and Continental food.
Chetak Circle (tel: 25132).

Lake Palace Hotel RRR

Excellent lunchtime buffet and à la carte dinners (Indian and Continental) in magnificent surroundings with live entertainment (see page 128). The only way to see inside this fabulous hotel is to eat here or stay here. Book ahead.
Lake Pichola (tel: 23241).

Shilpi R

Open-air restaurant serving all types of food, near the Shilpgram and Lake Fateh Sagar. Public access swimming pool.
Rani Road (tel: 60635).

CHILLI AND SPICE

There are three possible explanations of the name, curry. The Tamil word for sauce is *kari*; the *kari* leaf is a commonly used spice; and there is a North Indian dish, made with chickpea flour and buttermilk, called *karhi*. Curry as a dish was an invention of the Raj, however, and has nothing to do with real Indian food. The spice base used for proper Indian cooking is a *masala* paste, with a different mix of ingredients for each dish. Common spices include chilli, cloves, turmeric, cardamom, fenugreek, cinnamon, cumin, garlic, mace, nutmeg, coriander, tamarind, poppy seeds, saffron, caraway, ginger, peppercorns, asafoetida, mustard and kari leaf. Contrary to all popular belief, not all (good) Indian food is laden with chillies, although most dishes are highly flavoured. The Indians themselves would never expect to survive a vindaloo-strength blast every day.

Bread, vegetables and spices are the most important ingredients used for North Indian cooking

Every region of India has its own distinctive cuisine. In Delhi you will find them all and more. Some favourite dishes, such as South Indian *dosas* and *idlis*, the Moghul *biryani* and Punjabi *tandoori*, the Raj's peppery mulligatawny soup, the sweet Bengali *ras malai* and *kulfi*, Indian ice-cream, have become industry standards found in restaurants throughout India and the world.

On the whole, North India eats more meat than the south, while the carbohydrates are provided by a range of wheat-based breads, such as *nan*, *roti*, *paratha* and *puri*, rather than a constant diet of rice. *Mughlai* cuisine is the finest and richest on offer. The culinary legacy of the Moghul court, it blends Persian and Indian dishes and the very best of ingredients, cooking with yoghurt, almonds, raisins, and butter to create rich, luscious, creamy sauces and delicately perfumed rice. It is rarely very hot. Marinated and grilled meat and vegetable *kababs* are typically Muslim. Dry *tandoori*, again marinated and cooked in a clay oven, only arrived in Delhi from the North-West Frontier after Partition in 1947, but has been enthusiastically adopted. Traditional, Rajasthani food, with breads and spicy vegetarian dishes, can be hard to find.

Puddings are not a standard part of the normal menu, but do exist. Most are

milk based and immensely sweet. Halva-type sweets are made to celebrate festivals. They are elaborately decorated, even with wafer thin sheets of real, edible silver and gold. Meals are usually ended with a mouth freshener and digestive, such as aniseed or *pan*, a cocktail of betel nut and flavourings such as cloves, cardamom, fennel, lime or the red catechu bark, all served in a heart-shaped *pan* leaf.

Hotels and Accommodation

*P*eople build great hotels in India, it's maintaining them that's the problem. No one seems to notice as the dust builds up, and the cockroaches start nesting. As a result, the industry is definitely two-tier, with a top class of superbly run international standard hotels – and everything else. The trick of living well at an affordable price is knowing where's good this season, or even this month. The good news is that Rajasthan definitely has more than its fair share of good hotels and guest houses and the sophistication of Western requirements is beginning to rub off.

Up-market hotels

The service in high-quality hotels is impeccable. You will also get a marble bathroom, 24-hour room service, satellite TV, messenger services, shopping arcades, travel agents, gyms, beauty salons, a swimming pool and anything else you can think of. In Delhi, there are custom-built business hotels, with fully functional secretarial services, conference facilities etc. Elsewhere, businessmen are catered for by the 5-star de luxe tourist hotels which offer all the service, most of the facilities and much more atmosphere. Rates are calculated in US dollars and there is an extra 10 per cent luxury tax.

Heritage Hotels

Eighteen of India's 21 official heritage hotels are in Rajasthan. The state also has over 600 forts and castles, over 1,000 palaces and numerous royal mansions and *havelis* ripe for conversion. A massive development programme with heavy government subsidies is underway, aimed at having 100 heritage hotels by the year 2000. The current brochure lists those operating and a list of properties for

Lake Palace Hotel, Udaipur

CENTRAL BOOKING

Between them, these chains own almost all the luxury and mid-range hotels in the region.

Ashok Corporation

The state-run chain of the India Tourism Development Corporation, with hotels in Delhi, Agra, Bharatpur, Jaipur and Udaipur. They come in three types – dirt cheap and dirty; mid-range, reasonable price and very comfortable; and all-singing all-dancing super-luxury. Check which you are booking.

Jeevan Vihar, 3rd Flr, 3 Sansad Marg, New Delhi 110001 (tel: 332 4422/311 621/311 607; fax: 343 167).

Oberoi Hotels

Luxury and mid-range hotels in Delhi and Agra.

c/o Oberoi Hotel, Dr Zakir Hussain Marg, New Delhi 110 003(tel: 436 3030 ; fax: 436 0484). UK – tel:

(0800) 515 517 (toll-free); fax: 0181-789 5369. USA – tel: (800) 5–OBEROI (toll-free), (212) 752 6565; fax: (212) 758 7367.

Rajasthan Tourism Development Corporation

Bikaner House, Pandara Road, India Gate, New Delhi (tel: 383 837/381 884; fax: 382 823).

Hotel Swagatam Campus, near Railway Station, Jaipur (tel: 60586/70252; fax: 76245).

Taj Group of Hotels

Luxury/palace hotels in Delhi, Agra, Jaipur, Udaipur, including the Rambagh Palace and Lake Palace – the finest hotels of all.

Taj Mahal Hotel, Apollo Bunder, Bombay 400039 (tel: 202 3366; fax: 287 2711).

UK – tel: 0171-828 5909 (toll-free – (0800) 282 699); fax: 0171-834 8629.

US – tel (toll-free): (800) 44; fax: (402) 398 5484.

Welcomgroup/Sheraton

Luxury/palace hotels in Delhi, Agra, Jaipur, Jodhpur, Bikaner and Khimsar.

Maurya Sheraton, Diplomatic Enclave, New Delhi 110 021 (tel: 301 0101; fax: 301 0908). Toll-free booking: UK – (0800) 353 535; USA – (800) 325 3535.

The colonial Oberoi Maidens Hotel, one of Delhi's oldest

anyone interested in investing.

Among those already operational are some of the world's finest palace hotels, several beautifully converted minor palaces and castles, in town and in the bush, at rock bottom prices, and mansions and hunting lodges filled with dust and stuffed tigers. With so much fabulous atmosphere around, it seems a shame to stay anywhere else.

The sumptuously decorated Samode Haveli, a converted merchant's house

Mid-range Hotels

There is a real shortage of hotels in the Western 3- to 4-star category at a non-expense account price. There are a few, in the US$30/70 (single/double) price range, just below the luxury tax category. The architecture and range of facilities varies, but all are clean, comfortable, and well-run. Book well in advance during high season. Because of their scarcity, a few of the best are listed below.

Delhi: Oberoi Maidens (Oberoi), Ambassador (Taj); **Agra**: Novotel (Oberoi); **Bharatpur**: Forest Lodge (Ashok); **Jaipur**: Narain Niwas Palace (tel: 563 448), Samode Haveli (private; tel: 42407); **Jaisalmer**: Naryan Niwas Palace (private; tel: 2408); **Jodhpur**: Ajit Bhawan (private; tel: 37410); **Sariska**: Hotel Sariska Palace (private; tel: Sariska 222, Delhi 739 712, Jaipur 382 314); **Udaipur**: Shikarbadi (private; tel: 83200), Anand Bhawan (Rajasthan State Hotels, tel: 23256/28957).

Tourist Bungalows

Tourist bungalows date back to the Raj when a chain of government guest houses was set up for travelling administrators. These days, the architecture is usually mundane, very few are bungalows, but in some of the smaller towns, they really are the best on offer. In most places, however, they are being overtaken by a constantly changing flow of other smaller, pleasant guesthouses (see below). Run by the RTDC, tourist bungalows exist in almost every town and city in Rajasthan, they provide a very reasonably priced, rat-free environment with showers and fans that usually work and they are easy to find in a strange city. On the other hand, most are sloppily run and the cleanliness and food could definitely be improved. Prices vary from about Rs150–600 a night, dependent on location, type of room and facilities.

Other Cheap Options

You will need to do your homework to find other cheap alternatives. There are a great many cheap and very cheap hotels and guesthouses around. Some are wonderful, others poorly run but with such great atmosphere you can forgive them almost anything; many are so dire, you start itching as you walk through the door. Ask other travellers for suggestions. The rickshaw wallahs will try to steer you away from places that don't pay commission. Don't believe them when they say a place is full, or has gone down hill. On the other hand, if it really has, go and see their suggested place. It may be run by a cousin, but they have a good idea of what travellers want.

Always inspect the room before you agree to take it, including testing such basics as the flush, lights and fan, and making sure the bed has sufficient clean sheets. If there is anything wrong, ask for a handyman or cleaner to be sent up. You can usually get things sorted if you are persistent. Certain facilities, such as laundry, are available absolutely everywhere.

Ultra-cheap
The rather grim 'Indian' hotels are probably best avoided unless you are totally broke. A number of cheaper hotels also offer some dormitory accommodation and almost every railway station has retiring rooms, with dormitory beds and private rooms. Very handy if you are arriving late or leaving early. They are very popular and must be booked. Many of the larger temples run pilgrim hostels. The accommodation is spartan and the rules strict, but the cost is minimal.

Home Stays
Run by the RTDC, this programme, which places travellers as paying guests in a family home, is spreading rapidly and proving highly popular. The accommodation is usually comfortable and you have an excellent opportunity to get to know the local people. Ask the RTDC or local tourist offices for details.

There are RTDC tourist bungalows everywhere

On Business

*D*uring the Raj, India was used as a dumping ground for British goods. At independence, Nehru instituted a series of Five Year Plans, designed to make India as self-sufficient as possible. They have succeeded spectacularly. India can feed herself, and has a broad-based national industry. If there is little choice and the quality is sometimes poor, there is very little you cannot buy. (For more, see page 11.)

The last few years have seen a massive policy swing. The rupee has become partially convertible and India is slowly cutting the red tape and opening its doors to international business, although the emphasis is on investment, not imports. There is a vast and very cheap workforce, a huge range of traditional Indian goods which could be adapted for a Western market, and an increasingly large Indian middle class, looking to the West for new ways of spending money.

BUSINESS ETIQUETTE

Indians can usually pigeon-hole people easily and are uncomfortable with unknown Westerners, so take a good supply of business cards and answer their questions to put them at ease. The system is hierachical and the trappings of authority will help you maintain a necessary image, as will a formal approach. Western-style informality leaves people floundering. Women should have no problems in doing business.

DIFFICULTIES

The bureaucracy is stuck somewhere in the 19th century. It is cumbersome, infuriating and often totally unnecessary – but it does work, eventually. If you become totally bogged down, show up as a courtesy gesture, but take an Indian intermediary to do the actual negotiating on your behalf.

Caste involves very strict divisions of labour – and there are unions as well. No high caste person would ever dream of getting his hands dirty and if you ask a low caste person to give him an order, he will either ignore it or take offence. This creates massive overmanning, disrupted working and a social minefield.

There is corruption, but bribery is not universal and it is usually possible to do business legally. You may be faced with requests for *baksheesh* and two sets of figures, white money (the price on the invoice) and black money (the real price, or undeclared top-up). The government is trying very hard to crack down with harsh penalties for both parties.

Finally, Indians are very polite. They won't admit they haven't understood, will tell you only what they think you want to hear, and will not argue even if they think you wrong (although they may go and do what they wanted anyway). Always check things several times and put everything in writing.

BUSINESS MEDIA

There are three main English-language business papers, the daily *Economic Times* and *Financial Observer* and the bi-monthly *Business India*. The satellite television channels, BBC World Service, CNN and ZEE TV all do Asian business updates. See also page 184.

BUSINESS SERVICES

All high-level and government business is conducted in English. Interpreters between all Indian languages and most mainstream world languages are available in Delhi and, to a lesser extent, in Jaipur. Elsewhere, you would do best to take someone with you. Delhi and Jaipur both have specialist business hotels, with full secretarial facilities, but most luxury hotels offer some services.

The Pragati Maidan exhibition ground in Delhi can house conferences from 15 to 11,000 people. The BM Birla Auditorium in Jaipur can also handle large groups. All the five-star hotels, including the palace hotels, offer small-scale conference facilities.

Thomas Cook Delhi (see page 188) offers a specialist service to incoming businessmen, including organising conferences and incentive travel.

BM Birla Auditorium, *Statue Circle, Jaipur 302005 (tel: 382 267/381 594; fax: 41763)*. Conference facilities, full secretarial and courier service.

Freelance Interpreters and Translators, India (FITI), *(tel: 604 416/550 7884/550 7808/646 4413)*. Delhi-based association with Spanish, French, German, Russian and English on offer.

Pragati Maidan, *Bhairon Road, New Delhi (tel: 331 7824)*.

Transtechnique, *F-7, South Extn-1, New Delhi (tel: 694 013; fax: 469 4558)*. Interpreting, translation, conference facilities and printing.

COMMUNICATIONS

For telephones, see page 187. Public fax and telex machines are available only in the major hotels and central post office/telecommunications centres. Because the internal phones are so difficult, the lines are so bad and the

Multi-national business is booming in Delhi since the lifting of investment restrictions

possibilities of mislaid/forgotten messages so great even if you do get through, it is worth using a fax or telex to make or confirm any arrangements. Several courier companies have offices in Delhi.
DHL Worldwide Express, *D1/B Ashirwaad Building, Green Park, New Delhi (tel: 686 4590/1)*.

OFFICE HOURS

See page 185.

FURTHER INFORMATION

Confederation of Indian Industries (CII), 23/26 Institutional Area, Lodi Rd, New Delhi 110 003 (tel: 462 9994; fax: 463 3168/462 6149).

Federation of Indian Chambers of Commerce and Industry (FICCI), Federation House, Tansen Marg, New Delhi 110 001 (tel: 331 9251).

PHD Chambers of Commerce, PHD House, opp. Asian Games Village, New Delhi 110 016 (tel: 686 3801; fax: 686 3135) and 9-A Connaught Place, New Delhi 110001 (tel: 332 7421).

Culture Shock India by Gitanjali Kolanad (published by Kuperard) is a very useful guide to Indian custom and etiquette, including sections on how to do business and how to live and function in India and still retain your sanity.

Practical Guide

CONTENTS

Arriving
Camping
Children
Climate
Clothing
Conversion Tables
Crime
Customs Regulations
Documents
Electricity
Embassies
Emergency Telephone Numbers
Health
Insurance
Language
Maps
Media
Money Matters
National Holidays
Opening Hours
Organised Tours
Pharmacies
Places of Worship
Post
Public Transport
Security
Senior Citizens
Student and Youth Travel
Telephones
Time
Tipping
Toilets
Tourist Offices
Travellers with Disabilities
Useful Addresses
What to Take

ARRIVING

Most people fly into Delhi. The area is landlocked and its only international land border (with Pakistan) is closed. There are good road and rail connections with most other areas of India, and Delhi, Agra, Jaipur, Jodhpur, and Udaipur are all equipped with domestic airports offering regular scheduled services. Negotiations are currently in progress to open up the military airport in Jaisalmer to civilian traffic.

Travelling by Air

Air India (international) and Indian Airlines (domestic) are both state-run airlines. However, many major international airlines have flights into Delhi, most offering good deals, so shop around. International flights are usually timed for convenience at the other end and arrive in or depart from Delhi in the small hours of the morning. Remember to reconfirm all international flights at least 72 hours before you travel.

Domestic services have been deregulated relatively recently and there is a growing number of operators. For the moment, Indian Airlines is still the largest. The standard is improving, but internal flights can be pretty hit or miss, with regular cancellations, over-booking, and delays.

Few Western travel agents are prepared to risk making the booking without a disclaimer. Wait until you arrive and use a local travel agent who should know what's happening. Indian Airlines offer a US$400, 21-day unlimited travel pass, only really useful if you are planning to cover the entire sub-continent.

Indian police are smart, well disciplined and formidable

Indira Gandhi Airport
This is the main international gateway to India. There are currency exchange counters in the baggage reclaim hall, expensive duty-free shops on arrival and departure, and tourist information and hotel booking desks in the arrivals hall.

The easiest transport into town is pre-paid taxi – get a ticket from a booth in the arrivals hall. There are also very cheap, very slow buses, again bookable before you leave the terminal building.

On departure, your baggage must be security checked and sealed and you must pay your departure tax before check-in.

The international terminal is 9km southwest of the city, off Gurgaon Road; the domestic terminal is 2km closer. Airport information: 545 2011/329 5181; flight information: 301 7733 (international), 329 5434 (domestic).

Departure Tax
Airport/departure tax is due on all flights, payable before check-in – Rs40 for domestic services, Rs300 on international flights. Local currency and cash only, so keep enough back.

Airline Offices
Almost all airline offices are in or around Connaught Place.

Air India
Jeevan Bharati Building, 124 Connaught Place (tel: 331 1225).

Air France
Scindia House, Janpath (tel: 331 0407).

British Airways
DLF Building, Sansad Marg (tel: 332 7428).

Indian Airlines
PTI Building, Sansad Marg (tel: 371 9168); 24-hour reservation desk – Safdarjung Airport.

KLM
Prakash Deep, Tolstoy Marg (tel: 331 1747).

Lufthansa
56 Janpath (tel: 332 3310).

CAMPING
There are few facilities for camping in or near the towns and accommodation is so cheap, it really isn't worth it. All camping equipment is supplied during desert safaris.

CHILDREN, see pages 160–1.

CLIMATE

The tourist season runs from mid-September to April, peaking from November to March. It can be chilly in Delhi and the mountains in mid-winter, but throughout this period, it is usually hot and sunny through the day, while the evenings are pleasantly cool. The desert can feel bitterly cold at night because of the massive temperature variation.

Through May and June, the temperature climbs steadily under a sweltering sun to almost unbearable levels until early July, when the monsoon arrives with torrential rains, thunder storms and, all too frequently, floods. This lasts to early September. The desert collects few of the monsoon rains, but the season is characterised instead by high winds and sand storms.

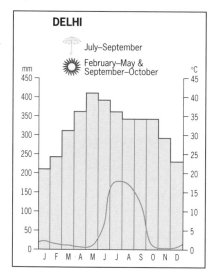

DELHI

July–September

February–May & September–October

CLOTHING

Clothes should be portable, durable, comfortable and all-encompassing. Women should avoid short skirts, shorts (culottes are an excellent alternative) and anything sleeveless; men can wear baggy shorts but may need long trousers for temple visiting. Loose-fitting clothes in natural fibres or mixes, eg cotton or poly-cotton, are by far the best suited to the heat. Dress is usually informal, but take at least one reasonable outfit (including a tie for men) for smarter restaurants. You will probably need a lightweight jacket or sweater for evenings. Long sleeves and trousers help fend off mosquitoes. Wear comfortable shoes or sandals that allow your feet to breath.

It is easy and incredibly cheap to get laundry done but your clothes will take a hammering. They are usually sent down to the river with the *dhobi-wallah* and beaten on the rocks. If you have anything fragile, wash it yourself, so try to take things that don't need ironing.

It is possible to get clothes made in a matter of hours. The Indian *shalwar khamiz* (pyjama suit) is ideally suited to the climate and very comfortable.

CONVERSION TABLES

India uses the metric system. There is a slightly different method of counting high numbers. One *lakh* is 100,000 (written as 1,00,000); one *crore* is 10,000,000 (written as 1,00,00,000).

CRIME, see **Security**, pages 186–7.

CUSTOMS REGULATIONS

200 cigarettes, 1 litre of alcohol and gifts to the value of Rs 600. Declare more than US$10,000 and any expensive electrical items such as camcorders and computers which will be checked on departure. Clearance is needed for the export of antiques, and export of most animal products such as crocodile skin, tortoiseshell and ivory is prohibited.

DOCUMENTS
A valid passport and visa are needed.
Apply *in person* in your home country or
expect delays. Allow 2 days to 2 weeks.
Most tourist visas are valid for six
months. Check the current situation with
the Indian Embassy in your country.
Visa applications can be made at the
following addresses:

Australia
Indian High Commission, 3–5 Moonah
Place, Yarralumla, Canberra ACT 2600
(tel: 62–733 3999).
Canada
Indian High Commission, 325 Howe
Street, 1st Floor, Vancouver, British
Columbia.
New Zealand
Indian High Commission, 10th Floor,
Princess Tower, 180 Molesworth Street,
Wellington (tel: 4–73 6390).
UK
Visa Department, Indian High
Commission, India House, Aldwych,
London WC2B 4NA (tel: 0171 836
8484).
USA
Indian Embassy, 2107 Massachusetts
Avenue NW, Washington DC 20008
(tel: 202–265 6653

ELECTRICITY
220–240 volts. Most plugs are 2 round
pin. Power cuts are frequent in places,
but short-lived. Take a torch.

EMBASSIES
Indian Embassies Abroad
Australia
3-5 Moonah Place, Yarralumla, ACT
2600 (tel: 62–733 3999).
Canada
10 Springfield Road, Ottawa K1M 1C9
(tel: 613–744 3751).

Conversion Table

FROM	TO	MULTIPLY BY
Inches	Centimetres	2.54
Feet	Metres	0.3048
Yards	Metres	0.9144
Miles	Kilometres	1.6090
Acres	Hectares	0.4047
Gallons	Litres	4.5460
Ounces	Grams	28.35
Pounds	Grams	453.6
Pounds	Kilograms	0.4536
Tons	Tonnes	1.0160

To convert back, for example from
centimetres to inches, divide by the number
in the the third column.

New Zealand
10th Floor, Princess Tower, 180
Molesworth Street, Wellington (tel: 4–73
6390).
UK
India House, Aldwych, London WC2B
4NA (tel: 0171–836 8484).
USA
2107 Massachusetts Avenue NW,
Washington DC 20008 (tel: 202–939
7000).

Foreign Embassies in India
Australia
1/50-G Shantipath, Delhi
(tel: 688 8232/687 2035).
Canada
7/8 Shantipath, Delhi
(tel: 687 6500).
New Zealand
50-N Nyaya Marg, Delhi
(tel: 688 3170).
UK
50 Shantipath, Delhi
(tel: 687 2161).
USA
Shantipath, Delhi (tel: 60 0651).

EMERGENCY TELEPHONE NUMBERS
Police: 100
Fire: 101
Ambulance: 102

HEALTH
India is home to almost every disease known to mankind. Follow the advice, have the shots, and carry a good medical kit, including sterile needles, and if something does go wrong, don't shrug it off. Above all, don't panic. Few travellers suffer more than minor stomach upsets.

AIDS and Hepatitis B
Both diseases are widely prevalent. Stay celibate or take a good supply of condoms, and use them.

Food and water are India's main health hazards

Cuts and scratches
Even minor wounds can fester easily. Clean them thoroughly, use an antiseptic and keep them covered. Treat regularly and if they become infected, take antibiotics.

Inoculations
There are no statutory requirements, however it is sensible to have inoculations for typhoid, tetanus, polio, tuberculosis, yellow fever, meningitis A and C (for Delhi and the north), and hepatitis A. The cholera vaccine is ineffectual, so is not recommended.

Hospitals and doctors
The quality of medical care varies enormously. The standard of medical training is good but facilities are often poor. Most hotels have an English-speaking doctor on call. If you need hospitalisation, insist on one of the big teaching hospitals or a private clinic, which are as good as any in the world. Ambulances will always take you to the nearest place, so try and stay conscious!

Insist on using your own needles and do everything short of dying before you have a transfusion of local blood. Ask your friends to help and contact your embassy. Some have blood banks, others keep a register of clean donors.

Malaria
Malaria is endemic and can kill. You must take prophylaxis. Check with a good travel clinic or tropical diseases hospital, start two weeks before you leave and keep taking the pills for four weeks after you get home. If you show flu-like symptoms at any time within the next six months, ask for a malaria test.

The carrier, the female anopheles mosquito, only comes out at night. The best prevention is to avoid being bitten, so cover up well, use a good repellent, spray the room, use a coil and, if possible, a mosquito net.

Stomach bugs

These are almost obligatory, but most are minor and will disappear within a day or so. If possible, suffer for the duration, give up on food except basics like dry toast, chapatis and yoghurt, and drink plenty, with a little sugar and salt to help replace essential minerals. Immodium will plug you up, but is not a cure. If it lasts more than a couple of days, consult a doctor.

Never, never drink water unless from a bottle you have seen opened or you have sterilised it yourself. This includes ice and street-stall fruit juices (diluted with tap water). Check out any restaurant for basic cleanliness (although Western standards of hygiene are a forlorn hope). All cutlery and glasses should be clean and dry, and wash your own hands before you touch food. Stick to fresh-cooked, hot foods. Never eat any fruit you can't peel and make sure that snacks are properly and securely wrapped.

Sunburn and heat-stroke

Much of this area is desert, and all of it is very hot. It is extremely easy to burn and dehydrate. Wear a hat, use sunglasses, and a high-factor sun block and carry water with you. Drink far more than you think you should need. First symptoms of heat-stroke (overload of the cooling system) include a headache, nausea and blurred vision. Get into a cold bath and call a doctor.

Rabies

Don't touch any animals, domestic or wild. Rabies is one of a host of infections they may carry. Should you get bitten or scratched, insist on full rabies treatment immediately. If you wait until symptoms develop, it's too late. If travelling more than 24 hours from medical help, get immunised before leaving.

For further advice, contact the Thomas Cook Travel Clinic (see page 188).

INSURANCE

Good, comprehensive travel insurance is essential. Too many things can go wrong here. Your policy should cover air evacuation, third-party liability, legal assistance, loss of possessions (including finances and passports), cancellation and/or delay of travel. Adventure sports and motorcycles are rarely covered by standard policies, so double-check and, if necessary, pay for an extension.

Signs of success – one of Bundi's more thriving businesses

LANGUAGE

India has 14 official and 65 recognised languages and about 550 dialects, of which Hindi is the most widely spoken, especially in this region. English is the language of government. Rajasthani is split into two closely linked dialects, Mewari in the south and Marwari in the north. In the very remote villages, there are a host of additional dialects and tribal languages belonging to minority ethnic groups like the Meena and Bheels. A few words of Hindi can be useful and will always be appreciated but almost everybody speaks some degree of more or less eccentric English, and if they don't, the person eavesdropping will willingly help out.

MAPS

Several people publish good maps of Delhi, Agra, Rajasthan and Jaipur, the best probably being the *Discover India* series (TT Maps & Publications). The RTDC do a good free tourist map of Rajasthan. For all other towns and cities, you will be almost totally reliant on sketch maps.

MEDIA

India is very media oriented. The main national English-language dailies include the *Times of India, Hindustan Times, Hindu, Indian Express* and *Statesman*. All major cities have their own English-language daily and there are numerous weekly or monthly news magazines. There are also three TV channels – one Hindi, one English, one regional (all government controlled). Satellite Star TV, with BBC World Service TV, and CNN are available in most good hotels. Numerous local and national radio stations broadcast in a range of languages including English. BBC World Service and Voice of America are both available. International newspapers, *Time* and *Newsweek* are available at major hotels, a few days late and very expensive.

MONEY MATTERS
Currency

The *rupee* is divided into 100 *paise* (rarely used except as *baksheesh*). Keep a good supply of small notes and coins. No one ever has change and it is difficult to break notes. Check all notes carefully. Most are disgustingly worn and moth-eaten, but if too badly torn, they become invalid.

Exchange facilities

It is illegal to import or export *rupees*, but there are 24-hour exchange facilities at the airport. Change money at the hotels or agencies where possible. Not all banks handle foreign exchange and the procedure can be time-consuming and wearisome. The black market rate isn't worth the risk. Keep your exchange forms. You will need one to change money back into hard currency or pay for hotel rooms or air tickets in *rupees*.

Cheques and credit cards

For safety, use well-known brands of US dollar or pounds sterling travellers cheques. Suspicious counter-clerks won't change anything they don't recognise. Major credit cards are widely accepted on the luxury circuit. Elsewhere, they are useless bits of plastic, so make sure you always carry enough cash to support yourself. India is still primarily a cash economy. An emergency supply of a few (cash) dollars can be helpful if you get into trouble away from the major cities.

Prices

The luxury end of the market works to international standards and prices (usually quoted in US dollars) and attracts 20 per cent luxury tax, on top of the usual 10 per cent sales tax. The tax structure is very complex and tax is never included in the price quoted. Out of package tourist land, prices plummet to Indian levels, which are rock bottom. The few fixed price shops always have signs saying so. Restaurants, hotels and market food stalls also work to fixed pricing. Elsewhere, you must haggle, with the first price quoted based on what they think you can afford. Accept that your bargain will still be twice as much as the price to an Indian – but it is also very cheap for you, so everyone is happy.

NATIONAL HOLIDAYS

Fixed public holidays – 26 January (Republic Day); 15 August (Independence Day); 2 October – Mahatma Gandhi's birthday; and 25 December (Christmas Day). There are a great many movable festivals, only some of which count as official holidays. These include Holi – the festival of colour (February/March); Good Friday (March/April); Buddha Jayanti – the day of Buddha's birth, enlightenment and attainment of nirvana (May/June); Janmashtami – Krishna's birthday (July/August); Dussehra – the defeat of the demon Mahishasura by Durga (a 10-day festival, two days of public holiday, September/October); Diwali – the festival of lights (October/November); Govhardhana Puja – for worshipping cows (November); Nanak Jayanti – birthday of Guru Nanak, founder of Sikhism (November). For the most colourful festivals, see pages 158–9.

OPENING HOURS

Opening hours tend to be very flexible, so don't treat those listed below as gospel.

Banks: Monday to Friday, 10am–2pm; Saturday, 10am–12 noon.

Government offices: Monday to Friday, 9.30am–5pm; Saturday, 9.30am–1pm.

Post Offices: Monday to Friday, 10am–5pm; Saturday, 10am–1pm.

Shops: Monday to Saturday, 9.30/10am–6pm (small shops and bazaars often open until at least 8pm).

ORGANISED TOURS

Huge numbers of Western tour operators offer tours including Delhi, Agra and Jaipur, fewer take you further into Rajasthan, and very few stir off the well-trodden path around the half-dozen major cities. Most of them stay at the same few palace hotels and do pretty much the same things. Shop around for price and also look at how long they give you at each stop. All too many whip you across India leaving barely enough time to breath.

Once in India, everybody is prepared to offer every conceivable version from the tatty coach trip to the luxury custom tour, even if it is not in their brochure. For day or half-day tours, stick with the tourist office who will either have a coach tour or can provide you with your own guide. For longer tours, use a reputable operator, such as Thomas Cook (see page 188). Everyone goes to the same places; the price variation will depend on whether the coach works, the hotel has bed bugs and the food is edible. For off-beat safaris, see page 144; for the Palace on Wheels, see page 29.

PHARMACIES

Pharmacies are marked by a green cross. They work long hours, but don't rely on a rota-system for 24-hour service. Out of hours, try the nearest hospital or clinic. You can get local versions of all common medicines, but anything specialised may be hard to find.

PLACES OF WORSHIP

There are Hindu and Jain temples and mosques in abundance. All the major towns have at least one Christian church. There is a synagogue in Delhi. Look in the phone directory or ask hotel reception for details.

POST

Post usually does arrive but can take months. Use a fax for urgent correspondence. Speed Post claims to guarantee delivery in Europe, USA and some other countries in 48 to 72 hours. Stamps are sold at most hotels as well as post offices. For *poste restante*, underline the surname as things can get lost by misfiling. Sending parcels can be really time-consuming as you have to get them sewn up and sealed, fill in the forms, get the form sewn on and queue several times over.

PUBLIC TRANSPORT

See pages 26–7.

SECURITY

India is fairly safe. There is a lot of petty crime such as pick-pocketing and sneak theft, and most women face a degree of irritating hassle, but violent crime is rare and the hassle is just that.

Always use a money belt for valuables and cash. Keep some emergency cash, a record of your travellers' cheques and credit cards, some spare passport photos, and a photocopy of the crucial pages of your passport (including the visa) somewhere separate. Don't leave baggage unattended at any time. If you can't avoid it, padlock it to something immovable. Watch out for sleight of hand tricks when other people are handling your money. Don't always trust other travellers. Above all, don't do drugs and never carry anything through customs for anyone. The penalties are harsh these days.

Police

Indian police are not the world's most sympathetic. Some are fine, but there is a lot of corruption and brutality around. If you need to claim on your insurance, you will have to produce a police report. Dress as smartly as possible, take someone with you as a witness, and make sure there is a written record of everything. If in doubt, or if you are arrested, get word to your embassy immediately.

SENIOR CITIZENS

There are discounts for Indian pensioners only, but prices are so cheap, it doesn't matter. Travel only between November and March, or the heat will be too debilitating and, unless you have enormous reserves of energy and stamina, take an organised tour or hire a car with a competent driver/guide.

STUDENT AND YOUTH TRAVEL

Most Western tourists to India are young, eager and, by their own standards, penniless. It is the perfect destination, with rock bottom prices, if you are prepared to put up with a degree of discomfort and dirt. Indian Airlines do a 25 per cent youth discount. There are no other youth discounts, but they aren't really necessary.

At the cheaper hotels and guest houses (see pages 174–5), you will lock into a system of like-minded travellers who love nothing better than to offer advice. Insurance and attention to hygiene are crucially important to budget travellers, and make sure someone always knows roughly where you are in case of emergency.

TELEPHONES

It is much easier to make a clear international call via satellite than it is to place a landline call to the next town. The internal phone system is extremely frustrating. Avoid it where possible.

Phone booths have sprung up almost everywhere recently, usually in the back room of a small shop. Look for yellow signs saying ISO (local), STD (long-distance), and/or ISD (international). Metered machines show how much you are spending. Pay at the end. If you need to book through the operator, you have a choice of regular (normally up to 1 hour wait) or lightning calls (still up to 30 minutes wait, and many times more expensive). India is on the Home Direct scheme for reverse charge (collect) calls and many charge cards, such as AT&T, BT and Mercury, are valid. For telex/fax, see page 177.

TIME

GMT + 5 hours 30 minutes. When it is noon in Delhi, it is 6.30am in London, 1.30am in New York and 4.30pm in Sydney, Australia.

Communication within India can be difficult

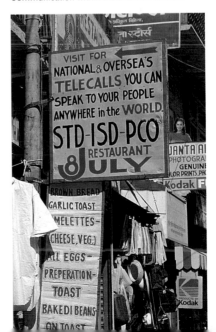

TIPPING

Tipping (as opposed to *baksheesh*, see page 30) is customary at more upmarket hotels and restaurants although many include a service charge, and a few rupees is plenty. Tip hotel porters and suchlike about Rs10–20. Station porters, taxi drivers etc officially work to set rates, but will always try to over-inflate the price. If you have had to haggle for anything, don't then spoil the effect by allowing yourself to succumb to the constant demands for more. Converting money back into hard currency in your head can make you feel cheap, but remember, anything you give goes into the local economy with local buying power. Be generous, you have a great deal more money than the Indians, but also spare a thought for other impecunious travellers coming along behind you.

TOILETS

Most places have Indian-style long drop toilets, although some have a few Western-style seats as well. The luxury market lives up to its name with splendid facilities and hot and cold running assistants. At mid-level, toilets are a bearable but unpleasant experience. At the lower end, they are scenes from hell. Public toilets don't exist, and if they do, you wish they didn't. Wherever you find something vaguely hygienic, grab the opportunity. Always carry with you your own supply of toilet paper and a small cake of soap.

TOURIST OFFICES IN INDIA
Government of India Tourist Office
88 Janpath, New Delhi (tel: 11–332 0005/8).
India Tourism Development Corporation
L-Block, Connaught Place, New Delhi (tel: 11–332 0331).
Delhi Tourism Development Corporation
N-36, Connaught Place, New Delhi (tel: 11–331 3637).
Rajasthan Tourism Development Corporation
Bikaner House, Pandara Road, India Gate, New Delhi (tel: 11–383 837/381 884).
Hotel Swagatam Campus, near the railway station, Jaipur (tel: 11–60586/70252).
Uttar Pradesh Tourist Office
Chandralok Building, 36 Janpath, New Delhi (tel: 11–332 2251/371 1296).
Other offices are listed under the relevant towns in the **What to See** section.

TRAVELLERS WITH DISABILITIES

Life is not impossible, but it is very difficult indeed. The airlines provide wheelchairs, the better hotels have lifts and a very few upmarket international chains provide basic facilities. Elsewhere, there is no provision, the country is so disorganised that advance preparation is virtually impossible, and most monuments are surrounded by steep steps.

On the plus side, labour is very cheap and the Indians are, by nature, kind. Expect to be almost totally reliant on muscle power. For more information, contact RADAR (the Royal Association for Disability and Rehabilitation), 12 City Forum, 250 City Road, London EC1V 8AF (tel: 0171–250 3222; fax: 0171–250 0212) or SATH (Society for the Advancement of Travel for the Handicapped), 347 Fifth Ave, Ste 610, New York, NY 10016 (tel: 212–447 7284; fax: 212–725 8253).

USEFUL ADDRESSES

THOMAS COOK
UK

45 Berkeley Street, London W1A 1EB (tel: 0171–499 4000)
As well as a travel service, this branch (worldwide head office) includes a visa service, travel clinic (open Monday to Friday, 8.30am–5.30pm for consultations and inoculations) and travel library.

INDIA
Delhi

Rishya Mook Building, 85–A Panchkuin Road (tel: 011–374 7404).
Hotel Imperial, Janpath (tel: 011–332 7135).
International Trade Towers, Nehru Place (tel: 011–642 3035).
Thomas Cook in India operate a wide variety of tours, both day trips and longer. They will also organise customised tours for individuals, business travellers, conferences and incentive groups. Travellers who purchase their travel tickets from a Thomas Cook network location are entitled to use the services of any other network location, free of charge, to make hotel reservations or to obtain free emergency assistance. In addition, any MasterCard holder may use any Thomas Cook Network location to report the loss or theft of their card and obtain an emergency card replacement as a free service under the Thomas Cook MasterCard Alliance.
Thomas Cook Travellers' Cheques loss or theft: +44 733 502 995 (reverse the charges).

INDIAN TOURIST OFFICES ABROAD
UK

7 Cork Street, London W1X 1PB (tel: 0171–437 3677; fax: 0171–494 1048.)

USA

30 Rockefeller Plaza, Suite 15, North Mezzanine, New York NY 10020 (tel: 212–586 4901/2/3/4; fax: 212–582 3274)
3550 Wilshire Boulevard, Room 204, Los Angeles, CA 90010 (tel: 213–380 8855; fax: 213–380 6111).

WHAT TO TAKE

Not everything on this list is crucial, but these things can help make life much more pleasant, especially if travelling cheaply. A good medical kit is essential. Notebook and pencil/pen; torch; sunglasses; wide-brimmed hat; small penknife with bottle opener; teaspoon; water bottle; your own cup or straws; universal bath plug (few basins have them); washing line and travel wash; toilet paper, tampons and condoms; inflatable pillow, eye mask, sheet sleeping bag and/or shawl to double as a blanket on overnight trains. A small element for boiling water in your room; tea bags, instant coffee and instant soup; a small pot of Marmite, Vegemite or other favoured food; muesli bars (an excellent meal substitute when ill, in transit, or during early morning starts); boiled sweets, for long journeys and making friends; film and batteries (these are available, but quality is limited and dubious). For the most suitable clothes to take, see page 180.

A
accommodation 172–5
  budget 174–5
  camping 179
  home stays 175
  hotels 172–4
  tourist bungalows 174
addresses, useful 188–9
adventure sports 162
Agra 10, 56–64
  environs 62–4
  Itimad-ud-Daulah's
    Tomb 57
  Ram Bagh Gardens 57
  Red Fort 58–9
  Taj Mahal 60–1
airports and air services
  178–9
Ajmer 65–7
  Adhai-Din-ka-Jhonpra 65
  Akbar's Palace 65
  Ana Sagar 66
  Dargah Sharif 66
  environs 67
  Mayo College 65
  Nasiyan (Soni) Jain
    Temple 66
  Taragarh (Star Fort)
    66–7
Akal Wood Fossil Park
  104
Akbar 54, 58, 62, 64, 65,
  130
Akbar's Mausoleum 64
Alwar 68–9
  Bala Quila Fort 68
  Cenotaph of Musi
    Maharani 68
  environs 68–9
  Government Museum 68
  Sagar 68
  Vinay Vilas (City Palace)
    68
Amar Sagar 104
Amber Fort (Amer) 94–5
  private apartments 95
  Sheesh Mahal (Hall of
    Mirrors) 95
  Shila Devi Temple 94
Ambika Mata Temple 132
Aravalli Hills 10
Ashoka 52
Aurangzeb 55, 130

B
Babur 54
Bairat 68–9
Baisakhi Temple 104
baksheesh 30
Balsamand Summer
  Palace 112
banks 184, 185
Baroli temples (Badoli) 86
beggars 30
Bharatpur 70–1
  environs 71
  Government Museum 70
  Keoladeo Ghana Bird
    Sanctuary 70, 140

Logarah (Iron Fort) 70–1
Bhensrod Garh Sanctuary
  141
Bhim Chauri temple
  complex 87
Bijolia temples 86
Bikaner 74–7
  Anup Sanskrit Library
    76
  Bhandasar Jain Temple
    77
  Bika Ji-Ki-Tekri 77
  Chintamani Jain Temple
    77
  environs 77
  Ganga Golden Jubilee
    Museum 74
  Junagarh Fort 74–5
  Lalgarh Palace 76
  old town 76–7
  Sadul Museum 76
  safaris 144–5
Bissau 146
brassware 149
Brindaban 64
Bundi 80–3
  84 Pillar Cenotaph 80
  Jait Sagar 82
  Kshar Bagh tombs 83
  Nawal Sagar 80
  old town bazaar 83
  Palace 81
  Raniji ki Baori 83
  Shikar Burj 83
  Sukh Mahal (Palace of
    Bliss) 82
  Taragarh (Star Fort) 81
  terraced garden 82
buses 26–7
business travel 176–7

C
camel breeding farm
  (Bikaner) 77
camping 179
car hire 26
carpets 148
caste 16, 138
Castle Bijaipur 144–5
Chambal River 80
Charbhuja 137
children 160–1
Chittorgarh 78–9
  Fateh Prakash Palace 78
  Gaumukh Kund (Cow's
    Mouth) 79
  Kalika Mata Temple 79
  Kumbha Shyam Temple
    78
  Mira Bai Temple 78
  Padmini's Palace 79
  Palace of Rana Kumbha
    78
  Vijai Stambha 78
  walls and gates 78
climate 180
clothing 180
conversion tables 180, 181
credit cards 185

cricket 162
crime and personal safety
  186–7
culture shock 30
currency 184
customs regulations 180

D
Damodra 105
Darrah Game Sanctuary
  86–7, 141
Dayel Bagh Temple 64
Deeg 71
Delhi 10, 34–53
  Air Force Museum 42
  airline offices 179
  airports 178–9
  Appu Ghar fairground
    161
  Ashokan pillars 52
  Baha'i House of
    Worship 36
  Bal Bhavan and National
    Children's Museum 161
  British Raj enclave 49
  Chandni Chowk (Silver
    Street) 48
  Connaught Place 47
  Craft Museum 42
  Fatehpuri Mosque 49
  Feroz Shah Kotla 51–2
  Gandhi Memorial
    Museums 42
  Hauz Khas 51, 52
  Hazrat Nizam-ud-Din
    Aulia 36
  Humayun's Tomb 36–7
  India Gate 46
  Indira Gandhi Museum
    42–3
  Indraprastha 50
  Jahanpanah 51
  Jain and Sikh temples
    49
  Jama Masjid (Friday
    Mosque) 37
  Jan Path 47
  Jantar Mantar 37
  Lakshmi Narayan
    Temple 37
  Lal Kot 50–1
  Lal Qila (Red Fort) 38–9
  Lodi Gardens 52–3
  Museum of Rail
    Transport 43
  museums 42–4
  National Gallery of
    Modern Art 43
  National Museum 44
  National Philatelic
    Museum 47
  Natural History
    Museum 47
  Nehru Memorial
    Museum and
    Planetarium 43
  New Delhi 46–7, 53
  Old Delhi 48–9
  Purana Qila 52, 53

Qutab Minar Complex
  44–5
Quwwat ul-Islam Masjid
  (Might of Islam
  Mosque) 44–5
Raj Ghat 45
Rajpath 47
Rashtrapati Bhavan/
  Secretariat Buildings 47
Safdar Jang's Tomb 45
Sansad Bhavan (Houses
  of Parliament) 47
Shah Jahanabad 53
Shankar's International
  Dolls Museum 43
Sonehri Masjid (Golden
  Mosque) 49
Tughluqabad 51, 52
Zoo 161
departure taxes 179
Desert National Park 104,
  140
Devi Kund Sagar and
  Cenotaphs 77
Dhebar 140
Dilwara temples 118
  Luna Vasahi Temple 118
  Mahaveer Swami
    Temple 118
  Parshwanath Temple 118
  Pittalhar Temple 118
  Vimal Vasahi Temple
    118
disabilities, travellers with
  188
driving 26
Dundlod 146

E
economy 11
Eklingji Temple 136, 137
electricity 181
embassies 181
emergency telephone
  numbers 182
entertainment 156–7
etiquette
  business 176
  religious 30–1
  social 30

F
Fateh Sagar 134–5
Fatehpur 146
Fatehpur Sikri 62–3
  Hiran Minar 62
  Jami Masjid 62
  palace complex 63
  Sheikh Salim Chishti's
    Dargah 63
festivals 158–9
  Desert Festival 158
  Diwali 159
  Dussehra 159
  Gangaur 159
  Holi 158–9
  Pushkar Mela 159
  Republic Day 158
  Teej 159

flora and fauna 142–3
  birdlife 72–3
  camels 144
  tigers 121, 122–3
food and drink 164–71
  chillies and spices 170
  'continental' food 164
  drinks 165
  eating out 166–9
  hygiene 183
  Indian cuisine 170–1
  menu reader 171
  street stalls 165

G
Gaitor 98
Gajner Sanctuary 77, 141
Gandhi, Mahatma 24,
  42, 45
Gaumukh Temple 118
geography of India 10–11
Ghandi, Indira 23, 42, 45
Ghandi, Rajiv 23, 42, 43,
  45
Gokul 64
Golden Triangle 6
golf 162
Goverdhan 64
Great Thar Desert 10
Guru Shikhar 118

H
Hadoti 80–7
  Bundi 80–3
  environs 86–7
  Kota 84–5
Hadoti Plateau 80
Haldi Ghati 136
havelis (Rajasthani
  houses) 146
health 182–3
  AIDS and Hepatitis B
  182
  cuts and scratches 182
  inoculations 182
  malaria 182–3
  medical treatment 182
  pharmacies 186
  rabies 183
  stomach bugs 183
  sunburn and heat-stroke
  183
health and fitness facilities
  162
history of India
  chronology 12–15
  Moghul emperors 54–5
  the Rajputs 92–3
hotels 172–4
  central booking 173
  heritage hotels 172–3
  mid-range hotels 174
  up-market hotels 172
Humayun 53, 54, 130

I
Indira Gandhi Nahar 11
inoculations 182
insurance 183

J
Jahangir 54, 65, 66
Jai Singh II 88, 99
Jaigarh Fort 99
Jaipur 88–91, 96–7
  Albert Hall 89
  Central Museum 89
  Chokri Sarhad (City
  Palace) 89
  city walls and gates 97
  environs 94–5
  Govindji Temple 97
  Hawa Mahal (Palace of
  the Winds) 90
  Ishvar Lat 97
  Jantar Mantar
  (astronomical
  observatory) 97
  Johari Bazaar
  (Goldsmiths' Market)
  97
  Lakshmi Narayan
  Temple (Birla Temple)
  90
  Moti Doongri 90
  Mubarak Mahal (Palace
  of Welcome) 89
  Museum of Indology 91
  Nahargarh Fort (Tiger
  Fort) 91
  Ram Niwas Gardens 96,
  Rambagh Palace 168
Jaisalmer 100–7
  Bada Bagh 100
  Badal Vilas (Mandir
  Palace) 107
  citadel 102
  city gates 102
  Dashara Chowk 102
  environs 104–5
  Folklore Museum 103
  Gadi Sagar (Gadsisar
  Lake) 103
  gun emplacements 106
  Jain temples 102
  Nathmal ki Haveli 107
  Patwon ki Haveli 107
  Rajmahal (City Palace)
  102
  safaris 145
  Salim Singh ki Haveli
  107
Jaisamand 140
Jait Sagar 82
Jal Mahal 98–9
jewellery 148, 154
Jhalawar 87
  Gagron Fort 87
  Jhalarapatan (City of
  Temple Bells) 87
Jhunjhunun 146
Jodhpur 108–13
  environs 112–13
  Government Museum
  112
  Jaswant Thada 110
  Meherangarh Fort 110–
  11
  safaris 145

Sardar Market 111
  Umaid Bhavan 112
  Umaid Gardens 112
jodhpurs 111
Junagarh Fort (Bikaner)
  74–5
  Anup Mahal (Dancing
  Court) 75
  Chandra Mahal (Moon
  Palace) 75
  Phool Mahal (Flower
  Palace) 75
  Sheesh Mahal (Mirror
  Palace) 75

K
Kailashpur 136
Kankroli 137
Kanoi 105
Karni Mata Temple 77
Keoladeo Ghana Bird
  Sanctuary 70, 140
Kota 84–5
  Chambal Gardens 84
  Chhatris 84
  fort complex 85
  Government Museum 85
  Hawa Mahal (Wind
  Palace) 85
  Jag Mandir 85
  Kishore Sagar 85
  Rao Madho Singh
  Museum 85
Kuldhara 105
Kumbhalgarh 132

L
Lake Rajsamand 137
languages and dialects 184
leatherwork 149
lifestyle 16
Luderwa 104–5
  Kalp Vrkasha (Tree of
  Imagination) 105
Lutyens, Sir Edwin 47, 53

M
Mahaban 64
Maharani-ki-Chhatri
  (Queens' Cenotaphs) 98
malaria 182–3
Mandakini Kund 118–19
Mandawa 146
Mandore 112–13
maps 184
  see also Contents
markets and bazaars 150–1
Mathura 64
media 176, 184
medical treatment 182
Menal Shiva temples 87
miniature paintings
  130–1, 149
Moata Sagar (Lake
  Moata) 94
money 184–5
  cheques and credit cards
  185
  currency 184

exchange facilities 184
  pricing structures 185
Mount Abu 116–19
  Adhar Devi Temple 116
  Baylay's Walk 117
  environs 118–19
  Government Museum
  116
  Honeymoon Point
  (Anadra Point) 117
  Nakki Talav 116–17
  Sunset Point 117
  view points 117

N
Nagda 136, 137
Nathdwara Temple 137
national holidays 185
national parks 140–1
  Bhensrod Garh
  Sanctuary 141
  Darrah Game Sanctuary
  86–7, 141
  Desert National Park
  104, 140
  Dhebar 140
  Gajner Sanctuary 77,
  141
  Keoladeo Ghana Bird
  Sanctuary 140
  Kumbhalgarh Sanctuary
  132
  Ranthambore 120–1
  Sariska 69, 140–1
  Sitamata Sanctuary 141
  Tal Chapper Sanctuary
  141
Nawalgarh 146
Nehru, Jahawarlal 22–3,
  43, 45

O
opening hours 185
Osiyan 113

P
packing tips 188
Padmini 78, 93
passports and visas 181
people and culture
  art 130–1
  caste 16, 138
  city life 40–1
  festivals 158–9
  lifestyle 16
  politics 22–3
  population 10–11
  Rajasthani traditional
  dress 85
  religion 18–21
  rural life 114–15
  textiles and jewellery
  154–5
  women in India 16, 17
pharmacies 186
photography 32
places of worship 186
police 186–7
politics 22–3

polo 162
population 10–11
postal services 185, 186
pottery 149
Prajabita
  Brahmakumari's Peace
  Garden 119
Pratap Singh 134, 136
public transport 26–9
Pushkar 67

R
rail travel 28–9
Rajasthan 10–11, 16–17
Ramgarh 87, 146
Ranakpur 132–3
  Chaumukha Temple 133
Ranthambore 120–1
  fort 120
  National Park 120–1
Red Fort (Agra) 58–9
  Akbar's Palace 58
  Anguri Bagh (Grape
  Garden) 58
  Jama Masjid 59
  Khas Mahal (Private
  Palace) 58
  Machhi Bhavan (Fish
  Building) 59
  Moti Masjid (Pearl
  Mosque) 59
  Musamman Burj 58–9
  Nagina Masjid (Gem
  Mosque) 59
  Shah Jahan's Palaces
  58–9
  Shish Mahal (Hall of
  Mirrors) 59
Red Fort (Delhi) 38–9
  Diwan-i-Am (Hall of
  Public Audience) 38–9
  Moti Masjid (Pearl

Mosque) 39
Museum of Archaeology
  39
Naubat/Naqqar Khana
  (Drum House) 38
Peacock Throne 39
private quarters 39
War Memorial Museum
  38
religion 18–21
  Hinduism 18–19
  Islam 20–1
  Jainism 21
rickshaws 26

S
safaris 144–6
  Bikaner 145
  camels 144
  Castle Bijaipur 144–5
  Jaisalmer 145
  Jodhpur 145
    Shahpura Palace 145
  Shekhavati 146
  Sajjan Garh (Monsoon
  Palace) 133
Sam Dunes 104
Sariska 69, 140–1
senior citizens 187
Shah Jahan 38, 55, 65, 66
Shahpura Palace 145
Shekhavati 146
shopping 148–53
  factory shops 150
  government emporia 150
  haggling 148
  markets and bazaars
  150–1
  opening hours 185
  what to buy 148–9
  where to shop 150–3
Sikandra (Akbar's

Mausoleum) 64
Siliseh Lake 69
Sisodia Rani ka Bagh 95
Sitamata Sanctuary 141
Soami Bagh (Dayel Bagh
  Temple) 64
sport 162–3
  adventure sports 162
  cricket 162
  golf 162
  health and fitness 162
  polo 162
  swimming 162
stonework 149
student and youth travel
  187

T
Taj Mahal 60–1
Tal Chapper Sanctuary
  141
taxis 26, 27
telephone and fax 177,
  187
textiles 149, 154–5
Thomas Cook offices and
  services 177, 188–9
Thomas Cook's India 6
time 187
tipping 187
toilets 188
tourist offices 189
tours, organised 186
travelling
  in India 26–9
  to India 178–9

U
Udaipur 124–9
  Ahar 129
  Bagore ki Haveli 126
  City Palace 126–7

dam wall 135
Dilkhush Mahal (Jovial
  Palace) 126
Dudh Talai Park 128
environs 132–3
Fateh Sagar 134–5
Folklore Museum 129
Gaitor 128
Government Museum
  126
Jag Mandir 128–9
Jag Niwas (Lake Palace)
  128
Jagdish Temple 128
Krishna Mahal 126
Lake Pichola 128
Manek Mahal (Ruby
  Palace) 126–7
Moti Magri (Pearl Hill)
  134
museums 129
Nehru Park 135
Pratab Smarak 134, 135
Sahelion ki Bari (Garden
  of the Maids of
  Honour) 135
Sajjan Niwas Park 129
Sanjay Garden 135
Shilpgram 135
Western Zone Cultural
  Centre 126

V
Vaishna Dwarikadheesh
  Temple 137
Vidyadhra ka Bagh 95

W
women in India 16, 17
women travellers 31

ACKNOWLEDGEMENTS

The Automobile Association would like to thank the following photographers and libraries for their assistance in the preparation of this book.

ALLSPORT UK LTD 163 (C Cole); **ARDEA LONDON** 143c; **BRIDGEMAN ART LIBRARY** 13, 54, 131a; **HULTON DEUTSCH COLLECTION** 22/3, 24; **D LAWSON/WWF UK** 122/3, 123; **NATURAL SCIENCE PHOTOS** 140, 141 (K Jarayam); **NATURE PHOTOGRAPHERS LTD** 72b (W S Paton), 141a (H Van Lawick), 142 (E A Janes), 143a, 143b (S C Bisserot), 143d (H Miles); **PICTURES COLOUR LIBRARY LTD** 127b, 171; **M SHALES** 80, 95b, 135, 138; **SPECTRUM COLOUR LIBRARY** 64, 89, 110; **TONY STONE WORLDWIDE** cover; **ZEFA PICTURES LTD** 103.; The remaining pictures, in the AA PHOTO LIBRARY, were taken by Douglas Corrance. The author would like to thank the following people and organisations for their assistance in the preparation of this book: the Rajasthan Tourism Development Corporation; Lalit Panwar; Jairaj Singh Chauhan; Surendra Singh; Henry Ledlie and the staff of Thomas Cook, Delhi; Oberoi Hotels; Taj Hotels; Indian Railways; Dr Dandapani of SD Enterprises, London; the India Tourism Development Corporation; Jennifer Shales; Jimmy and Ali, the best rickshaw-wallahs in Jaipur.

CONTRIBUTORS

Series Adviser: Melissa Shales   **Designer:** Design 23   **Verifier:** Judy Sykes   **Indexer:** Marie Lorimer